The
Heretic's
Handbook

A Contrarian's Guide to Modern Life

To Carly Comitino
Wishing you joy and
"light" throughout your life.
With All Best Wishes

M. A. Soupios

outskirtspress
DENVER, COLORADO

Outskirts Press, Inc.
http://www.outskirtspress.com

ISBN: 978-1-4787-1090-5

Outskirts Press and the "OP" logo are trademarks belonging to Outskirts Press, Inc.

PRINTED IN THE UNITED STATES OF AMERICA

For Aliana

*The world is kept alive only by heretics:
the heretic Christ, the heretic Copernicus,
the heretic Tolstoy—Yevgeny Zamyatin*

*Doubt is not a pleasant condition, but
certainty is absurd—Voltaire*

Convictions are prisons—F. Nietzsche

Contents

Preface

Recently, Aliana, my four-year-old granddaughter posed a series of unnerving questions that got me thinking. Out of nowhere she turned to me one day and asked, "Papou [grandpa] are you getting old?" to which I responded, "Yes." At this point she immediately began to wear a troubled expression on her face and said, "I don't want you to die." My initial response to her came purely as an attempt to allay her concerns. I said, "I don't want to die either, sweetheart, but don't worry, everything is fine." I noted my response did little to diminish the fretful look she continued to signal. I eventually told her that, with God's help, I planned on being around for a good long while and that we would have many happy times together in the future.

But would we? This brief exchange brought home to me two powerful points. First, the loving generosity of her concern for my life. This put a tear in my eye almost immediately. Odd how rapidly that ocular dew can appear. Second, her queries reminded me of one of those great disagreeable truths, the kind we work very hard to deny, viz., the terrible fragility and brevity of life. My granddaughter had, in a manner consistent with her age, put her finger on that great existential question. She had expressed, in the halting tones of a pre-schooler, Homer's ancient wisdom that we are all but "a generation of leaves." My puny efforts to assuage the dreadful reality of human finitude may have worked to some degree on her, but they did not work very well on me. I had to admit to myself that the assurances I had offered were in fact more than a bit hollow. Now, of course, I couldn't get into the philosophical aspects of all this with a four-year-old, so, in some sense, my encouraging words were appropriate to the situation. Still, part of me felt a sense of remorse at having engaged in an act of inter-generational fraud. In exchange for my granddaughter's guileless candor, I had offered platitude and euphemistic nostrum. The inequity of this discourse convinced me I owed her something more, which I proffer in these pages.

In what follows, I present a broad range of unorthodox assessments and commentaries which, be it hoped, will prompt subversive curiosities and a passion for forbidden truths. I would greatly prefer offering these provocative counsels to my granddaughter at a more mature point in her life when she might better grasp the spirit and content of my message. But as she herself reminds me, life is a precarious thing and we never know when the time will come to "shuffle off this mortal coil." It seems prudent, therefore, that I record these views now, as a kind of prospective endowment, while there are still a few grains of sand remaining in the hour glass.

Why, you might ask, would a grandparent wish to sow seditious seeds in the mind of his grandchild? At least in part the answer lies in an admonition offered by the British poet Alexander Pope who warned that "a little learning is a dangerous thing." As an alternative, he recommended we drink deep draughts from the Pierian Spring (the brook of knowledge), but to what extent does modern society encourage or even tolerate the sort of learned examinations advocated by Pope? I would argue that we are rarely urged to engage in anything approximating a thought-experiment, that the complexities of most social, political, and moral issues are routinely ignored in favor of a group-think mentality which not only accepts the unexamined life but prefers it. In great measure, this uncritical environment has been fostered by the siren song of "popular culture" (an increasingly oxymoronic term) and promoted by modern mass media. The effects are all too clear: jaw-dropping nonsense pretentiously parading as ripened insight. Simply put, much of what is commonly accepted these days as conventional wisdom is little more than an aggregate of sophistical doublespeak and mindless conformity, almost none of which can withstand serious scrutiny. It is necessary, therefore, that we encourage the iconoclast in the hope of advancing a benign heterodoxy and, further, that we approach such activities both as a duty and as a necessity. Only then will we be in a position to slough the straightjacket of prepackaged truths and manufactured conclusions society seems intent to impose. With these objectives in mind, I offer the following essays to my granddaughter and to anyone else interested in the emancipative benefits of heretical thinking.

M.A. Soupios

Truth

Whenever I consider the meaning of the word "truth" the first name that comes to mind is the Roman procurator of Judaea Pontius Pilate, who famously asked Jesus at his trial, "What is truth?" Pilate was not a philosopher; in fact he was a rather brutal governor much more concerned with power than with matters of verity. Still, the question he raised should, in a broad sense, remain our question. The problem is we routinely tend to neglect the importance of testing what we assume to be truth. We either conclude that whatever belief or value system we currently espouse is true or, worse still, passively endorse a standard of truth set down by others. In either case we are operating on automatic pilot to the extent that we mindlessly endorse that which we have failed to consider in any systematic way. The consequences of living a life under a misguided notion of truth can be very serious. Not only does it tend to guarantee assumptions and properties that lack foundation, it can also lead us to engage in reprehensible actions. In short, the potential negative effects of failing to periodically consider the meaning and implication of how we understand truth should not be underestimated.

How, then, is one to proceed with this important question? To begin with, one must start by respecting the complexity of truth. Too often people assume that truth is a simple thing, that it is nothing more than a facile process of arrangement. Unfortunately, there are few things in life that are as simple as all that. The problem with truth is that a great deal of it tends to reside in the gray zone between neatly delineated areas of black and white. In other words, truth tends to involve a good deal of nuance and intricacy that requires thorough, meticulous consideration. But this is not the way most people respond to the challenges of truth. When it comes to questions such as these, we are all guilty of reaching for conclusions that lack foundation and merit. This may be the result of slovenly mental habits or perhaps from the ease and convenience of simply endorsing the stale admonishments of received opinion. In any event, most people tend to ignore completely the Socratic maxim about how the unexamined life is not worth living. What I believe Socrates was getting at was essentially this: Arriving at the truth takes work. Claims to truth must be carefully weighed and sifted. Accordingly, you should make the following your general premise—*De ominibus dubitandum* (Have doubts about everything.) Moreover, one must understand that longevity of belief and practice is by no means a necessary guarantee of truth. Wrongheadedness, no matter how venerable or deeply rooted, still does not certify truth. The implication of all this would suggest that those who seek to lift the veil on truth must proceed cautiously and with open eyes, hearts, and minds. Above all, they must avoid the facile recipes society too often serves up as truth. When you are presented with truth on a platter, best to push yourself away from the table and seek sustenance elsewhere.

Given the complexity of truth, it logically follows that we must be suspicious of any who declare monopolistic possession of it. I suspect most of the assertions that have gotten the human race into trouble stem from this sort of claim. For one thing, those who profess such privileged ownership are typically the victims of simplistic, one-dimensional habits of mind. There are many people out there who are not capable, as matters stand, of appreciating life's complexity with the result that they willingly endorse versions of truth which are childishly, and even dangerously, naïve. This may not be quite as serious as it sounds. I would like to believe that under proper circumstances this category of deficiency is subject to remediation. Notwithstanding our many shortcomings, in principle nearly everyone is capable of learning and, therefore, capable of enhancing their understanding of truth. There are some, however, who may be beyond the therapeutic effects of education. I refer to the "true believers" who may be incapable of redemption by dint of ideological blindness. Here, I am reminded of an aphorism offered by Friedrich Nietzsche who warned that "convictions are prisons." These are the people who are most likely to unleash the greatest mischief in human affairs. They feel entitled to do so because only their ideas, assessments, and values reflect truth. What lies at the heart of all this is a terrible hubris that says "we, and we alone, are the custodians of truth." These are the arrogant souls who assert arcane understanding in such areas as race, religion, politics, economics. In fact, they suffer from a kind of compounded ignorance to the extent that they fervently believe they "know" that which they do not know. Any human environment interested in maintaining the pillars of civilized existence—peace, justice, compassion, understanding—must commit itself to exposing the dangers of a world in which ideological devotion is allowed to masquerade as truth.

At this point, you are no doubt filing formal charges against me for failing to specifically present a definition of truth. Fair enough. Let me begin with the following qualifications. First, I believe truth is genuinely complex and that part of the complexity relates to context and circumstance. This does not mean that I am a relativist. It simply means that one must proceed cautiously and in a manner that amply considers the many variables that collectively validate claims to truth. Second, I acknowledge that what I presently understand as truth remains a work in progress. I say this because I can clearly recall holding earlier conceptions of truth now entirely effaced as a result of insights gained through experience and, be it hoped, some ripening of mind. It is entirely possible, therefore, that the definition I offer now may change at some point in the future. I suspect, however, any alterations at this stage in my life will involve details rather than fundamental transformations.

Bearing these caveats in mind, I suggest that truth, in the largest sense of the word, is to be found among any constellation of values, principles, policies, and ideals that advance the well-being of humankind. By extension, truth does not lie in the depreciative and divisive judgments of those promoting *ex parte* "agendas." I refuse to believe in the interpretive integrity of those who condemn others based on race, ethnicity, gender, religion, or sexual orientation. How can these individuals possibly claim the status of "custodians of truth?" Rather than subscribe to a spirit of rebuke and reproach, these people need to heed the advice of Voltaire and enroll in the party of humanity. Therein, I believe, lie the best claims to veritas.

God

Historically speaking, few subjects have commanded more human attention and concern than the concept of God. In fact, concern about God has been one of the great formative forces behind human civilization, and, for many people around the world, its normative vitality has not diminished much at all, despite the counter-forces of modern secularism and technology. Perhaps the reason for this lies in some instinctive need in our species to envision a force more powerful and lasting than ourselves. The anthropologists seem to point in this direction to the extent that they claim no human culture has ever existed entirely devoid of some religious sentiment. Yet this raises a question regarding the basis of belief. Is the reason we "need" God a matter of our own frailties? Do we believe in God as a means of counteracting our fears, i.e., the manifold uncertainties of life? This is what Thomas Hobbes suggests in *Leviathan* when he states, "And this Feare of things invisible, is the naturall Seed of that, which every one in himself calleth Religion." Would we still maintain our beliefs in God were there no fear, pain, or suffering? I have no definitive answer for any of this, but I would strongly argue that examining one's premises in these matters is not blasphemy but rather a healthy exercise, however disconcerting the process.

In referring to the virtue of examining our religious assumptions,

I arrive at what I believe is one of the key issues regarding our considerations of God—to what degree are the characteristics and motives we attribute to God valid? On what grounds are we entitled to make knowledge claims about matters divine? One thing virtually all of the various faith traditions share in common is a tendency to speak authoritatively of their God. These assertions are often made side by side with contradictory claims that God's "mystery" is so vast and deep that mankind can never hope to penetrate the enigma. This reasoning has produced a special religious perspective known as negative theology, which says no human attribute can properly be affirmed of God. This idea, in one form or another, has been endorsed by everyone from Plato to Philo Judaeus to St. Paul and St. Thomas. But the point is, this caution to respect the mystery of God has consistently fallen on deaf ears. All those who practice a faith should be more than a bit amused with the voices of religious authority who speak of "the mystery of the Cross," the "mystery of Salvation," "the impenetrable mystery of God's design," etc. and then proceed immediately to a detailed discussion of the meaning and substance of these mysteries! If these questions are in truth "mysterious" then how are they so easily unpacked from the pulpit or from anywhere else? If these baffling issues prove subject to systematic decoding by human agency, then why are we still speaking of them in terms of mystery? Is it not possible that the Author of all things has elected to leave a few pages blank? Do our own frailties make us incapable of accepting that possibility?

There is yet another, more obvious issue we need to address, and it represents something much more fundamental than the logical inconsistency of assigning attributes to a divine entity we acknowledge as beyond our comprehension. I refer to the matter of God's very existence. In ascribing various characteristics to God prior to providing some evidence of God's existence, theologians of many faiths run afoul of a logical error known as *petition principia* (begging the question)—a fallacy first noted by Aristotle whereby a proposition which requires proof is assumed valid without adequate demonstration. In other words, we must be careful not to put the theological cart before the horse. Prior to declaring that God is unity, simplicity, incorporeal, eternal, immutable, omnipotent, good, etc., we have an obligation to present some evidence for God's existence. Eventually, Christianity did attempt to formulate various "proofs" in this regard. St. Anselm, for example, offered a famous "Ontological Argument" and St. Thomas advanced a more extensive five pronged demonstration based on the facts of motion, causality, contingency, relative perfection, and design. None of these attempts at "proving" God's existence are particularly compelling, notwithstanding the nimble ingenuity of these thinkers. We must accept the premise that, at the end of the day, religiously inspired rhetoric remains rhetorical, devotion and fervency notwithstanding.

So where does this leave us in the matter of belief in God? Does it deliver us to the threshold of atheism? Not necessarily. But it does suggest, in matters such as these, we must proceed cautiously and, above all, with a spirit of humility. To begin with, we are all entitled as rational beings to raise the kinds of questions suggested here. In the late 19th century a German historian named Jacob Burckhardt offered a rather sobering commentary on human gullibility. He said, "Reason for the few, magic for the many." One must not join the ranks of the many! If a school of thought, be it religious, philosophical, or political, insists that you become a credulous believer, i.e. oblivious, blind, unreflective, take this as a sign of disease and part company *post haste*. If, on the other hand, you find a faith community that is prepared to tolerate and even promote the inconvenient questions, a faith that is prepared to acknowledge that belief is an attempt to bridge things known and unknown, a faith that appreciates the only honest response to mystery is humble silence, this would be a group worthy of spiritual commitment because it does not confuse belief with comprehension.

Concerning the ultimate question—Is there a God?—what

human voice can respond definitively to this query? When it comes to an issue such as this, both the atheist and the theist are guilty of remarkable vanity in asserting their respective claims. What is my position? I have faith that there are powers at work in this world beyond human understanding. I can claim no knowledge of such things, yet I still believe, and if this suggests I am basing my faith on dubious foundations, I readily confess as much. For when it comes to questions such as these, I see merit in the paradoxical apothegm of an early Church father by the name of Tertullian who said, "I believe because it is absurd." And so, I content myself with a humble reticence and with the hope that at some point in the future this mystery will be revealed as only God can reveal it— be it hoped there is a God.

The Virtues of Solitude

The rhythm and cadence of modern life are such that we are rarely afforded an opportunity to enjoy a few quiet moments by ourselves. Instead, we are enjoined by clock and calendar to maintain a style of life intolerant of meditative opportunity. Ours is not to reason why. Our task is to simply join the ranks of the human herd and rush headlong toward goals and objectives that remain disturbingly unclear. Along with this crush and chaos, we are continuously assailed by a cacophony of widely distracting sounds that make even elementary thought processes next to impossible. In fact, I am increasingly convinced there is an inverse correlation between decibel level and quality of life. The more sound, the less comprehension, sensibility and intelligence. To the extent electronic dissonance has become the *lingua franca* of modernity, we may be denying ourselves a critically important insight, viz., that the greatest and most important sound of all is utter and complete silence. When does this culture ever turn down the volume? Where in the course of our daily lives do we make provision for a few quiet, contemplative moments?

Let's be clear about what is being suggested here. I believe there is a certain madness afflicting a good deal of modern life. It involves a perverse dedication to spend as much time as possible on autopilot, and by that I mean in front of the television set, a computer screen, or plugged into an iPod. It's as if we're afraid of hearing what our own inner voice might say to us, so we seek to drown it out by as much frivolous noise as possible. It seems to me this rejection of the introspective life can have at least two pernicious effects. First, it fosters a life lived at a most superficial level. Plato once spoke of a race of cave dwellers who were content to frame their existence based on shadows. There are real analogies here with the modern condition. Technologically speaking, we may have crawled out of the cave, but there has been little corresponding progress regarding truth, value, priority, etc. In terms of these considerations, our unwillingness to engage the forces "within" leaves us in precisely the same darkness Plato spoke of in Bk. 7 of *Republic*. We feverishly endorse phantom images at the expense of a higher and more genuine reality. Secondly, our attachments to things fast, loud, and unexamined will almost certainly serve to impoverish the human soul. Does anyone really doubt that a life lived as a witless, lock-stepping lemming results in anything other than pneumapathology, i.e., sickness of the spirit? Yet it appears that much of contemporary society is not only prepared to tolerate this illness, it is committed to promoting it by advancing notions of the good life that directly betray anything approximating spiritual hygiene.

Is there any antidote for this pandemic? How does one strip away the delusive skin culture encourages us to wear and re-engage the interior life? Given the oppressive weight culture often exercises in our lives, this is certainly no easy task. Still, I would argue, it is not impossible. The key lies in identifying an environment one might call the "sacred space" where a person can enjoy solitary discourse. Suitable locations might include a library, an unoccupied house of worship, or perhaps some setting where the healing and restorative powers of nature can be called upon to aid in the process.

In my case, the sacred space is located on a high bluff overlooking Long Island Sound. This is where I go, typically at the moment of "rosy-fingered dawn," to re-wire the workings of my soul. Here in my solitude far from the human swarm, I experience a unique reprieve, my personal version of the "flight of the alone, to the alone." A precious tranquility washes over me and I am transported beyond the mundane, the pedestrian, the vapid din of ordinary life. No siren's song here. Only the revitalizing effects of a solitary silence that informs and elevates. If, therefore, you seek the poetry of life, and this should become an important aspect of every human being's journey, know that you will never find it amid the discordant prattle of the multitude. Rather, you must locate your sacred space and retreat there as often as possible. Here you will discover the serene blessings of solitude as well as the Confucian wisdom— "Silence is a friend that never betrays."

Art and Beauty

My understanding of art and beauty is, by modern standards, highly heterodox. I am inclined to believe that these concerns have a critically important role to play in the *bios biotos*—the life worth living. I view them as much more than a source of entertainment, amusement, or financial opportunity. Art and beauty are serious matters to the extent art is the principal language of the soul. No form of human expression except worship is more spiritual. Indeed, I would argue that all great art is in fact a kind of aesthetic prayer, an attempt to explicate the sacred with chisel and brush. Evidence for these ideas is clearly available from the two greatest moments in the history of Western art—Greco-Roman antiquity and the Renaissance. The art of these periods reflects a purity of understanding and purpose that resulted in unparalleled achievement. For the ancient Greeks, art had a well-understood object. The aim was not simply to pay homage to Zeus or Apollo. The temples, statuary and paintings were designed to exalt and ennoble humanity as well. Here, I am reminded of a famous line from Sophocles' *Antigone* where he writes "many are the wonders, none is more wonderful than what is man." This paean to humanity was not unique to the tragic stage. It is a fitting summary of the prevailing cultural attitude of the ancient Greeks. In a sense, then, the goal of

Greek art was exhortative, i.e., it was an invitation to explore the "wonder" of human identity and, in particular, to appreciate the kinship between man and god. The specific strategy by which this was to be achieved lay in an art dedicated to representing "ethos," in other words, the universal character or essence of the subject matter. During its greatest moments, Greek art was consistently impatient with detail. Instead, it sought to represent humanity at its idealized best by blurring the lines between gods and men. In short, Greek art had a divinizing mission: it sought to make gods out of men by inviting humanity not to be content with an earthbound existence but to strive instead for Olympian heights.

These spiritualizing tendencies were also an essential feature of Renaissance art, but here the human focus is replaced by the enthusiasms of Christian belief. Although many of the great masters of this period continued to address themes derived from classical antiquity, the chief purpose of this art was the glorification of Christ. In this regard, the Bible provided an extensive range of subject matter: the Annunciation, the Nativity, the Baptism, the Ministry, the Crucifixion, the Resurrection, etc. The achievements of men such as Leonardo, Michelangelo, Raphael are immortal because they succeeded in addressing a universal spiritual longing that lies within the soul of virtually every human being. The specific method by which this was accomplished involved a conjoining of clearly held religious principles with an equally clear understanding of what constituted beauty. Armed with these insights, the Renaissance left an indelible mark on the history of Western civilization.

The point that needs to be recognized here, beyond all other considerations, is the commonalities shared by these two unique periods of artistic accomplishment. What unites Phidias with Bertoldo and Apelles with Botticelli, despite the passage of many centuries, is a clarity of cultural priority coupled with a deep appreciation for the mystery of beauty. Each society entrusted art with the remarkably important task of promoting the spiritual development of humanity because both civilizations understood that art has a special capacity to bestow a sense of the sacred.

I know this all sounds very ethereal, but I think there is evidence for a good deal of what I am suggesting. A few years ago I ordered a full-size cast of a famous statue sculpted by Praxiteles in the 4th century B.C. The original stands some seven feet tall and is found in the museum at Olympia. It represents the god Hermes in a playful scene with the infant Dionysus. After what seemed like an interminable wait, I finally received word that the statue had arrived at JFK airport. I collected several good friends, rented a truck and we were off. When we arrived, a huge crate was waiting at the loading dock. I explained to the forklift operator that I needed to open the box to make sure the piece had not been damaged in transport. When we finally unpacked the statue a remarkable thing happened. Upon seeing the sculpture the airport worker fixed his gaze on the face of Hermes and fell absolutely silent. I continued to examine the piece, anxiously checking for cracks and chips, but as I did so, the worker remained motionless and mute. Eventually his silence was broken by a shrill whistle directed to several of his co-workers who now gathered around the statue. Presumably, none of these men and women were college educated, and I seriously doubt any of them had ever heard names like Hermes or Praxiteles. Nevertheless, here they all stood marveling at a three-hundred pound piece of plaster. Unschooled though they were, these workers intuitively understood that this brief moment, interposed between their normal work activities, was something very special. They said things like "Wow, this is really cool, man;" and "How beautiful is that?" The lesson I took away from this encounter is simply this: Artistic beauty is a kind of meta-language capable of speaking to every human being. You do not need an art history course to engage in this variety of experience because the context is so powerful and fundamental to the human spirit. And one other point. Despite our vastly different backgrounds, all who stood on that loading dock were, for those few minutes at least, colleagues. Distinctions of gender, race, and educational level were completely irrelevant. All of these divisive distinctions meant nothing in the presence of beauty's magic. However briefly, we had all become joyful co-celebrants in an aesthetic ecumenism. What a wonderful occasion, something I will always cherish.

The degree to which modern art has disconnected itself from the historical foundations of Western art cannot be overstated. A key feature of this disassociation, made roughly a century ago, was the idea that art need not have anything to do with beauty. I believe the motive here was historically determined, and I fully understand the sense of disillusionment and hostility many artists felt toward the dark paths modern society seemed to be taking. Industrialization, urban squalor, social alienation and, above all, the unprecedented horror of WWI contributed to a spirit of profound disenchantment. Under these conditions, how could art continue its traditional preoccupations with beauty? If the world had become ugly, did not art have an obligation to mirror the disfigurement? In particular, there was a cause to "Epatez la bourgeoisie," i.e., shock the middle class out of its mindless lethargy.

Let me summarize my views here in the following manner— the motives were pure, the methods misguided. What many artists seemed not to have recognized is beauty's transcending significance for humankind. It has a transportive quality capable of creating the critical separations periodically required to restore human sanity. In truth, what this era needed was more beauty, not less. It needed an art that was not content merely to protest modern absurdity but was dedicated to reminding man of what is highest and best in the human spirit. Along these same lines, it is important to note an observation made by the literary critic Lionel Trilling, who warned that there is indeed such a thing as bad art and that artistic expression of this type may have the potential for habituating us to falsehood. In other words, it could be that modern art's protests may have had the opposite effect to their intended purposes. Instead of shocking modernity out of its delusions, it may have reinforced some portion of the absurdity by advancing the despairing notion that beauty's purifying virtues are now beyond our grasp.

In addition to severing the historic connection between art and beauty, modern art also lacks a guiding cultural principle. Whereas the ancients sought to apotheosize man and the Renaissance endeavored to hallow the Savior, modern art is uniquely devoid of over-arching purpose. This deficiency is by no means specific to the modern artistic community. Rather, it reflects a much larger shortcoming common to modern culture as a whole, viz., a debilitating confusion in matters of value and worth. Simply put, the Zeitgeist of modernity is unbridled subjectivism, a fully predictable result in a culture that has come to question its own credentials. Great art, the art capable of evoking sacred experience, requires a system of fundamental principles and ideals to guide its activities. In the absence of some canonical precept, art inevitably tends to degenerate into an anarchic relativism where the exalted ego of the artist reigns supreme. Here, everything becomes permissible because art is now understood as whatever an alleged artist says it is—a virtual guarantee of artistic malpractice. Needless to say, the opportunity for fatuous absurdity under these conditions is truly unlimited. Increasingly art has become incapable of separating itself from the insignificant, the sensational, the frivolous, the vulgar. More importantly, it is no longer willing or able to reveal aesthetic truth and mystery. The only thing art can do, given its profligate giddiness, is offer a wild profusion of forms, movements, and schools (e.g. abstract expressionism, pop art, kinetic art, super realism, performance art, etc.) For some, this spasm of artistic expression is a positive sign, a healthy and vibrant fecundity. In reality, these are merely the chaotic experiments of a culture depressingly devoid of rudder and compass. And, of course, we have a term for all of this, for a culture devoid of critical artistic assessment. The word is nihilism.

So, my advice is to remain severely circumspect when it comes to assessing modern art. Remember, genuine art does not need to be explained, justified, or promoted. The Louvre's Winged Victory is in no need of silken words from some art critic anymore than it requires some extended narrative in a museum catalogue. It has a language of its own which speaks powerfully and unmistakably to every human soul that takes the time to listen. This is the point made by Tom Wolfe's work *The Painted Word*, and he is absolutely correct. In the event, then, that you encounter some huge canvas that seems indistinguishable from a drop cloth, or a series of saffron "gates" festooning the byways of Central Park, or a huge mound of clothing tossed periodically like some enormous textile salad, remind yourself of Hans Christian Andersen's emperor. Be assured, your incapacity to perceive the artistic virtue in what you behold is not a shortcoming for which you are responsible. If there is any bourgeois philistinism operating here, it lies with those who spuriously rap themselves in the mantle of artistic genius. In sum, understand that many of the manifestations of self-centered inventiveness known today as modern art are often interesting curiosities. But, also know, they are best described as "events," "amusements," "happenings," etc. rather than "art" because real art is a noble and serious endeavor whose good name and weighty purposes should not be profaned by narcissistic pageantry and commercial contrivance.

Creature of a Day

Mortal! Know this well.
You are bound to an awful brevity.
Hades, the stone-hearted creditor, claims you
And all who wear the fleshed tunic.
No prayer, no billow of incense, no tallith smartly worn
Can dull the blade of Atropos' merciless shears.

This little poem was prompted by an article I read about, of all things, a tree. It seems a lightning storm recently destroyed a certain bit of foliage in Big Tree Park, Florida. So what? This sort of thing happens all the time. True enough. But this was no ordinary tree. It was an enormous bald cypress which stood 118 feet tall with a diameter of 18 feet. What struck me, however, was not the tree's size but its age. The experts tell us this colossal evergreen was 3500 years old! Think about that for a moment. When the wheel first arrived in Great Britain about 500 B.C., this tree had already stood for a thousand years. When Jesus went to the cross, this tree was more than fifteen-hundred years old! In the face of this astonishing antiquity, it was impossible for me not to consider the depressingly abbreviated timeframe we are all allotted as human beings. It was also impossible for me not to feel some sense of resentment or injustice at all this. Why should this insentient mass of cellulose enjoy an existence more than forty times my life expectancy? By what right does this arboreal colossus get to live for millennia while I revert to dust in three-score ten or there abouts?

I know it sounds silly to begrudge a tree its longevity, but I think the questions raised by the terrible brevity of human existence are important and need to be examined. I also think we tend to shrink from this type of analysis given the bitterness of the subject matter. To avoid this task, however, would be an act of conceptual dishonesty, a sin against our obligations as rational beings. We must, therefore, consider the narrow limits of our existence and do so with an eye toward how our meager time might best be spent.

When we are born into this world it is as if an hour glass is turned upside down and the sands begin to run. Of course, no one thinks along these lines amid the celebrations of a new life. For that moment, at least, pink or blue ribbons obscure the presence of father time and all that he implies. As the child grows, this obfuscation continues as part of the blissfulness of youth which includes a fundamental indifference to chronological considerations. For the young, chronology is a non-issue. Time seems like a boundless commodity, and the inconveniences of old age, things like illness and debilitation, are the afflictions that affect "others." Slowly, however, the bloom of youth fades and we begin to understand that we enjoy no special immunity when it comes to the great temporal vortex. With each diminishing capacity we are compelled, however grudgingly, to admit that there is a clock with our name on it. Increasingly, we experience an uncanny anxiety about our existential condition. Our physicians tell us everything is fine, but still the sense of angst within us continues to mount. At the same time, this unspecified foreboding is compounded by the realization that human life is not only dreadfully concise but fragile as well. One bad gene, a moment's distraction behind the wheel, a morsel of undercooked food, and suddenly the Pale Rider is upon us!

Finally, we reach a stage where the most terrifying sound in life is the pitiless ticking of a clock—any clock. Indeed, all references to time eventually become premonitory. Those candles on the cake, that obituary page, may not pertain to you specifically but they nevertheless become signposts of your own mortality, ciphers that read "memento mori."

As I said, none of this seems quite fair to me but there is a much larger irony attached to what I've said so far. Not only are we indentured to a remarkably brief life span, that's bad enough, but we are also the only biological entities on this planet that are fully aware of our inevitable demise. When our fourteen-year-old Rottweiler lay dying near the entranceway to our home she was still accepting food from family members literally moments before she was euthanized. There was no cognitive process in any of this, nothing to indicate awareness that her time was up. What I saw instead was a canine illustration of a Cartesian automaton, an animal responding mechanically to food stimulus. As far as she was concerned, this was not some climactic moment, not a situation that should impede her normal zeal for eating.

Whenever I recall this scene I think of the poet Thomas Gray who observed that "ignorance is bliss." My point in all this is simple—we enjoy no such bliss. When it comes to death and dying we bear a special burden. Awareness of our own finitude is a uniquely human dilemma that is not only inescapable but omnipresent. Now, we all know people who strenuously attempt to deny this reality. Their efforts can take a variety of forms, everything from mega-doses of vitamins to plastic surgery to cryogenic storage. To one degree or another, however, all of these efforts must be seen ultimately as gestures of existential "bad faith." In the end, of course, these comedic attempts to have youth linger a while longer are all for naught in the face of Cronos's remorseless decree. Throughout our lives, and particularly as we get older, we are called upon to attend various consummation rituals for friends and family (wakes, funerals, memorials). On some level of our consciousness, it is impossible to deny what these rites represent: dress rehearsals for our own dissolution. And it is this understanding that constitutes a special malignancy of the human condition. No tree, no animal is aware of its own inexorable extinction. This is the Sisyphean boulder that we alone roll in life.

How, then, shall we approach the ugly business of human finitude? There is no easy answer to this question, and certainly no answer that can possibly apply to all people and all circumstances. But let me begin by pointing out that we should never allow the many chronometric devices at our disposal to deceive us into thinking that we own time. In truth, it is precisely the opposite—time owns us. I think it is very important to acknowledge this candidly as a starting point in any attempts to map out a life strategy. With this in mind, I offer my first point, which is obvious enough. Make the most of the time you have at your disposal. To be clear, I am not suggesting you follow the sybaritic encouragements of the Assyrian King Sardanapalus, who famously said we should eat, drink, and be merry because everything else is not worth the snap of a finger. There is more to life than this gormandizing counsel would suggest and certainly greater forms of joy than a full belly. Celebrate your time with friends and family. Engage in meaningful work, and by that I mean activities that not only earn you a living but provide opportunity for reflection and self-development. In addition, take every opportunity to render assistance to your fellow human beings. This will lend depth and meaning to your life in remarkable ways, ways that most people cannot even begin to imagine. If, for example, there is a charity you believe in, write a check. If there is a food pantry that you know does good work, make a donation. If there is a scholarship fund that helps change young peoples' lives, contribute as much as you can. Understand who the true beneficiary is in all these situations. It is not the organization that receives the money. The true reward always accrues to those who bestow.

Thus far my advice has focused on some rather concrete measures but I also believe the specter of non-being makes necessary some consideration of a much more abstract idea, viz., "authenticity." Perhaps the best way to explain this word is to imagine a life lived in honest, genuine, legitimate terms. Think of an individual in whom self-deception and fraud hold little or no sway, a person prepared to confront whatever life offers in a defiantly courageous manner—even in the shadow of death. Here, I believe the observations of Martin Heidegger have considerable merit. Human existence, what he calls Dasein, remains incomplete and untrue without a forthright consideration of death. Like it or not, death is our constant companion throughout life, and as bitter as this inconvenient truth may be, we should not allow it to distort or falsify our lives. Yet this is precisely what so much of modern culture is dedicated to doing. Rather than encouraging an unambiguous examination of this most fundamental of all questions, society offers anesthesia. It attempts to convince us that there is no reason for concern, much less studied reflection. In effect, we are told to keep on whistling as we walk as rapidly as possible past the graveyard. In doing so, however, we guarantee for ourselves an inauthentic existence, a life which leaves us in a state of spiritual deficiency because denial such as this diminishes and demeans our status as human beings.

Admittedly, it is difficult to speak of death's virtues. The very idea seems ludicrous on its face. There is a sense, however, in which one can legitimately think along these lines. By honestly including death in the equation of our lives we affirm our worth and value as human beings. How? Because death provides the opportunity to demonstrate the authenticity of our existence. It is our chance to reveal a special worth even in the face of forces which we can never hope to deter or defeat. I think Dylan Thomas was aware of this when he counseled us not to go gently "into that good night." I also believe the ancient tragedians appreciate the same point when they encourage us to militantly resist life's malice as part of the means by which to earn the cognomen *deinon* (wondrous). Dignified defiance is an opportunity to demonstrate our value as something more than simply "creatures of a day." We alone grasp the mandatory retirement program fate has assigned our kind. Through defiance, however, we can register our status as something superior to the harsh forces that conspire against us. Perhaps this is our compensation for having to bear the terrible truth of life's brevity. In any event, death is our chance to express what is sublime and indomitable in the human spirit, an opportunity neither flora nor fauna can ever know.

Black America

For many years as a teenager and young man, I was convinced there was something deficient and wrong about people of color. My views reflected all of the stereotypic insularities of white, middle-class suburbia. According to this particular imbecility, Blacks were the source of crime, instability, and social disruption in society and needed to be marginalized as much as possible. They were the alien presence in America, the "other" that made our streets unsafe and who parasitically cost white America millions in social services. Who needed these people? This was the leitmotif of my family, my neighborhood, and my culture growing up in the 1950's and 1960's. Unfortunately, although white people are less inclined to manifest these biases today, there remains a malignant residuum in our society, a lingering reservoir of fear, stupidity, and ugliness we would rather sweep under the rug than address forthrightly.

During much of the civil rights movement I was attending high school and college. In looking back upon those times the only word I can offer as a description of my capacity for social analysis is "primitive." By that, I mean misguided, monolithic, brutish. My views regarding this struggle were entirely disfigured by the animosities I felt in my heart toward the Black community. The remarkable thing about all this is the fact that these sentiments, as strongly held as they were, were based on absolutely nothing. I had virtually no personal experience with Black people. There were none of them in my school, none where I lived, virtually none anywhere in my life. Yet by some inimical osmotic process, I had become convinced these were bad people and that the civil rights movement was evidence of their iniquity. Of course, I made no distinction whatsoever between non-violent demonstrations and militant Black separatism. To my way of thinking, every person of color who stood up and demanded his rights had a black glove on his right hand and a gun in his pocket—Medgar Evers or Huey P. Newton, they were all the same to me. I honestly believed the only thing these people really wanted was a chance to take it to the streets, to destroy white people's property and to walk off with everything that wasn't nailed down. And so it was, in April of 1968, when I learned that Martin Luther King had been murdered, that my first reaction was he had gotten what he deserved. He was a troublemaker, a rabble-rouser who spent his time traveling from one Southern city to another sowing the seeds of discord. He had encouraged Black America not to stay "in its place," and he had paid the price for his disruptive message.

Today, as I reflect upon the views I held back in my salad days, I feel a combination of embarrassment and shame—sentiments of contrition I now accept and value as symptoms of a long overdue sanity. Moreover, I am able to trace the precise event that engendered my eventual awakening. It occurred during my first year of graduate school. It was there that I came across a correspondence that stirred me from a dark, ignorant slumber. In one of my classes the professor distributed a packet of required reading materials. Contained therein was Martin Luther King's letter from the Birmingham City Jail. This essay, which was written in April of 1963, changed everything I thought I knew about Black people and the civil rights movement. It was my exorcism, the means by which the unclean spirits were cast out. I rapidly came to see these were not the words of some violent provocateur. He wasn't calling for social anarchy as a means of advancing the cause of his people. He spoke, instead, about non-violence, brotherhood, Christian discipleship, and he did it all in a beautiful, passionate narrative that came from deep within his heart. This was not a bad man, nor was he an enemy of white America. In fact, he may have been the best friend white America had. His death was a catastrophically unjust episode in the moral and social history of this country. He undoubtedly had more to say and more to teach, more lessons in spiritual probity to offer. It was my great good fortune to run across this missive. Dr. King was responsible for the scales falling from my eyes.

More than forty years have passed since I first read King's Birmingham letter. Where are we now in matters of civil rights, economic justice, racial equality? I suspect most white people would agree significant progress has been made while considerably less enthusiasm would be offered by those of color. White America seems to take a certain pride in reminding the world that a Black man sits in the oval office. This is taken as a sign of the nation's racial maturity, as evidence that the days of racial bigotry and intolerance are no longer part of the American landscape. What white America conveniently neglects in these self-congratulatory exercises are the placards portraying Barack Obama as an ape and assassination threats against President Obama four-hundred percent higher than they were against his white predecessor. These are hardly data suggestive of racial enlightenment.

So where do we stand, realistically speaking, in terms of race relations in America? Certainly progress has been made. At the very least, the various statutory exclusions have been erased and access to education and jobs have become more equitable. Still, no one should delude himself into thinking there is no work left to be done, that Martin Luther King's dream has been achieved. It is one thing to expunge the Jim Crow legislation, but altering the hearts and minds of white America is an entirely different and far more difficult matter. Attitudinal change, I mean something beyond the smarmy lip service of pseudo-liberalism, is a massively complex and tedious process. No one in white America should be complacent about any of this. No one in white America should be patting himself or herself on the back—not yet, my white brothers and sisters, not yet.

I base these observations on thirty-five years worth of interaction with African-American students in my classes. What these experiences have taught me is that while the racial gap has narrowed, there is still an awkward, painful, debilitating division between white and Black in this country. By way of illustration, I can offer dozens of advisement sessions in my office where young people of color have come to review their grades or to discuss career options. Typically, these sessions are permeated from the outset by a palpable sense of apprehensiveness. I am not referring to the normal status fissures that routinely distance a student from a professor. No, this is something very different, something much deeper and more insidious. These kids walk into my office in silence. They deposit themselves before my desk and wait to be told where to sit or stand. I always instruct them to sit in a chair close to my desk but despite closing any physical gap in the hope of creating some sense of accessibility, the body language invariably remains rigid and, above all, there is scant eye contact. This last point is the thing that bothers me the most. I purposely fix my gaze directly at their young eyes and they never fail to look away, or, more specifically, to look down. This is particularly true of the young Black men with whom I deal, more so than Black women. I believe this is the case because Black men have historically been a particular target of cultural emasculation. Even more so than Black women, this is the group white society has belligerently sought to keep on the plantation. What I see in my office every week is the ugly residue of this mentality. No matter how earnestly I attempt to reach out to these kids in the hope of kindling that I-thou relationship, the barriers stubbornly persist. What this suggests to me is that on some level of their psyches I am still "whitey" and a potential Lester Maddox in sheep's clothing. In a few cases, after several years of trust building, I am pleased to report real relationships do emerge. But the fact that it takes me two years to accomplish something I can routinely achieve in one semester with a white kid speaks volumes as to the depth of suspicion and pain still harbored by a significant portion of this nation.

There is an old saying about how time has the capacity to heal all wounds. Is there something we can do to accelerate the healing? One thing that comes to mind and that I am convinced is crucial to curing the racial discord of this country is the issue of poverty. Back in the 1960's, amid much bellowing and ballyhoo, America declared war on poverty. It was presented as a noble crusade dedicated to ending the suffering of the "other" America and to extending the dream of opportunity and prosperity to everyone, regardless of race. And what were the results of this lofty combat against the forces of economic deprivation? Well, if there really was a war on poverty, it was a war we clearly lost. In fact, we were routed, driven off the battlefield in headlong retreat. Fifty years after our declared intent to eliminate this societal scourge once and for all, we have never had more people in need. Perhaps most disturbing of all, the gap between rich and poor continues to widen, yet any proposal to increase the minimum wage in this country is met with howls of protest by the corporations and their congressional minions. The reasons why this "war" failed include ill-conceived public policy and gross mismanagement of resources, but, in the final analysis, these causes are, etiologically speaking, superficial and secondary. The fundamental reason why the campaign against privation failed relates to a misconception relating to poverty itself. Poverty is not simply an economic issue. It is not merely a matter of minimum wages and gross adjusted annual incomes. At its base, poverty in America is ultimately a problem of societal attitude. Is the society prepared to tolerate poverty or not? The answer seems to be that the majority of Americans are willing to accept a significant number of poor as long as they remain as distant and as "invisible" as possible. I base this conclusion on the tenor of our public discourse where substantive measures to address the poverty issue are immediately met with charges of "social engineering" and "class warfare." Ironically, these injunctions are frequently registered by individuals who profess deep attachments to the tenets of Christianity. Apparently they have misinterpreted Christ's words when he observed "the poor you will always have with you." As far as I can tell, this saying was not intended as an encouragement to maintain the ranks of the impoverished. What affluent Christians should instead take from the NT is Christ's instruction to the rich man who is told to sell what he has and give it to the needy. Much of the reason why poverty remains an incongruous blight on a nation as rich as the U.S. is the grotesque hypocrisy of many god-fearing men and women. These alleged pillars of the community who piously assemble each week at their houses of worship are perhaps best designated "ornamental" believers. They sing their hymns, recite their prayers, bend their knees at the appointed moments but at the same time they have no compunction whatsoever in ignoring the wretched existence of millions. What these good folks seem not to understand is that when a faith fails to command thought and deed then there is no faith, that in order for a faith to be real it must be part of lived experience.

This brings me back to my point about attitudes. Poverty is a kind of referendum on what a people see as permissible levels of human suffering. In very poor nations this level will, perforce, be high. But in societies where there is great abundance and yet tolerance for suffering nevertheless remains high, then the society in question is in desperate need of reexamining its economic, moral, and spiritual credentials.

Now what has all this discussion of poverty to do with the racial divide in America? I would argue there is more of a connection here than the obvious truism that many people of color are poor. What needs to be remembered is the impact poverty has upon American society. To begin, poverty should be seen for what it is, a thief. It steals human potential, human fellowship, and human dignity. It should be noted, the theft to which I refer works a reciprocal evil on poor and non-poor alike. Even those who remain secure in their economically privileged enclaves are still diminished by the presence of those incapable of securing a decent quality of life. This is so because poverty creates the sort of distances that encourage stereotypic thinking. The "poor" are reduced to an abstract category. They become a faceless mass of needy devoid of hopes, dreams, and constructive aspiration. Society sees them as an unfortunate cost of doing business, a kind of cultural write-off, the debit side of the ledger. In the process of marginalizing the poor, the thinking of affluent America often falls victim to a pernicious circularity. Most of the fear and animosity whites feel toward Black America are the effects of poverty rather than some innate feature of Black identity. I suspect nothing more powerfully reinforces the racial prejudices of white America than the images of inner city poverty. But what many white people do not understand is how their own biases foster and sustain the environment that engenders white anxieties in the first place. The relative ease with which this cycle can be broken is seen by the Black person who climbs out of poverty. Equipped with some education and a decent job, the ghetto stereotype of a doo-rag wearing street thug begins to fade along with the obstacles to inclusion. Now the person of color becomes a colleague, a neighbor, and even a friend. There is only one conclusion that can be drawn from all this, viz., poverty is the chief villain in America's racial quandary. Were we to reduce this pathogenic feature of our culture significantly, I suspect a great deal of the fear, hatred, and injustice that prevents America from fulfilling its promise would begin to disappear.

Eradicating the disease of poverty is a long-term proposition requiring a concerted effort on the part of all Americans. Among other things, it will necessitate new organizations, new programs, and new public policies—none of which will be easily or quickly forthcoming. What, if anything, can an individual do to promote racial harmony in this short-term as larger political and economic mechanisms are in the process of mobilizing? Here again, I advance a proposition concerning attitudes. As inherently complicated as race relations are in this country, the complexity is greatly compounded by a presumption of understanding on the part of white America. I offer myself as an example of the problem. At the ripe old age of sixteen, I was convinced that I understood African Americans, the civil rights movement, the Black leadership, etc. This breathtaking vanity led inexorably to a series of misguided conclusions that eventually hardened into full-blown racism. My mind remained entirely closed in these matters for years because I presumed to possess a kind of "gnosis" or special, esoteric insight. I uniquely grasped the meaning of racial phenomena in this country and any views to the contrary were, therefore, worthy of peremptory dismissal.

A mentality such as this is obviously lethal to anything approximating rational assessment. But, in addition, by assuming that a white person could really understand the meaning and substance of the Black experience in America, I mirrored the tendency of whites to presumptuously claim insights in matters completely alien to their lives. Simply put, no white man or woman, no matter how well-intended, should ever presume to understand the pain and indignity suffered by Black Americans. With very few exceptions, there is neither cognitive nor psychological foundation for any of their assumptions. What white community in this country can claim to have endured three hundred years of slavery, lynchings, and constant racist reminders that they are not fully or properly human? I would also extend this same caution to gentiles who claim to possess insight as to what the Shoah represents for Jews. How can anyone else outside the Jewish community understand what it means to be a target for complete annihilation?

In all such cases, we need to abide by an approach prescribed by the ancient Skeptics who advocated "epoche," or suspension of judgment. In other words, resist the urge to infer, conjecture, surmise, and conclude. In conferring with the marginalized, bring an open mind and a generous heart to the conversation. Remain receptive and respectful toward those who have experienced a quality of life you were blessed not to have known. And remember, when you hear some well-heeled member of the country club set recently returned from eighteen holes of golf confidently declaring he "feels the pain" of those society has rendered invisible, that these are the kind of glib, self-approbative pronouncements that continue to get in the way of racial justice in America. Judge less, my friend, empathize more.

The True Friend

Amid the hurly-burly of modern life there seems to be precious few occasions to reflect upon the meaning and value of a true friend. Too often, we simply apply the label "friend" in a most unsystematic and cavalier manner with the result we sometimes find ourselves widely betrayed by those we saw as trusted confidants. I believe this tendency to misidentify genuine friendships has become increasingly common in our society for reasons I will explain. Before doing so, however, there is a conceptual framework I believe any person interested in this subject would be well advised to consider. The antiquity of this perspective should not be an obstacle to our endorsing its logic. This is because friendship is one of those fundamental categories of human experience that transcends the specificities of a given time and place. In addition, there is the stature of the individual who proposed what follows, a man who's name remains authoritative in nearly all categories of philosophic speculation—Aristotle.

One of Aristotle's most influential works is the *Nicomachean Ethics*, a kind of "how to" manual for a properly lived life. Among other things, this treatise reflects a common Greek tendency to prioritize the "resources" necessary for happiness. Among the many elements one requires to construct a life worth living, Aristotle designates friendship as indispensable. In fact, he spends the better part of two chapters emphasizing the critical necessity of friends. In the course of his analysis, Aristotle distinguishes various categories of friendship. One of these is what he terms utility or accidental friendships in which people are bound together based upon a mutual usefulness. Relationships such as these tend to be highly unstable and typically fail to endure. The reason for this is traceable to the transient foundations of the relationship. According to Aristotle, utility is not a permanent quality but is subject to rapid and dramatic change as circumstances alter. It is best, therefore, to think of such relationships not as true friendships but as merely a special form of commercial alliance.

Genuine friendships are an entirely different matter to the extent they involve a depth and purity of sentiment completely absent in affiliations based on utility. In describing these relationships, Aristotle speaks of "love" as a special adhesive and key distinguishing feature of a real friendship. The content of this love is defined in terms of what an individual desires for his associate. A true friend wishes the good of the other as an end in itself. In other words, friendships are not business propositions. They are not investment opportunities aimed at paying some future dividend. Instead, Aristotle speaks of a friend as a second self, or, more poetically, as a relation in which two people "share the same soul." In addition, Aristotle insists upon one further component in his description of an authentic friendship, viz., a moral disposition on the part of both individuals. Those who lack moral discipline, people described by Aristotle as *akratic* (incontinent), are incapable of participating in the kind of relationship Aristotle defines as a friendship. Specifically, they are deficient in regard to certain critical aspects of character which tend to render friendship impossible. For Aristotle, then, there is an inextricable connection between being friends and being good.

Now, for most people, any reference to an ancient author, even one with Aristotle's credentials, immediately raises questions of relevance. What possible significance could the ideas of a man living in the late 4th century B.C. have for today? At best, he deserves treatment as a kind of historical curiosity; at worst, he merits consignment to the dustbin. As typical as these views may be, they are entirely ill-founded because they arrogantly assume that we moderns alone have anything insightful or important to say. In point of fact, Aristotle's analysis of friendship can legitimately be seen as a valuable antidote for many of modernity's opaque views on the subject. Take, for example, his analysis of utility friendships. The British historian Thomas Carlyle once observed that the sole connection between men in his day (19th century) had become the cash nexus. There are many obvious signs that Carlyle's observation is even more valid today than it was in the 1800's. Aristotle's dissection of true fellowship is a powerful reminder, particularly in an age of market economics, that business relations are a completely distinct species of human affiliation and should never be confused with friendship. Not only is this point of capital (no pun intended) significance for those engaged in commercial endeavors, it also reminds us of an even more important premise, viz, the qualitative infrequency of friendships. The sinews of friendship are not derived from mutual self-interest or from the judicious construction of a legal document. Relations such as these are purely situational, explaining their remarkable fluidity and the ease with which today's business partnership becomes tomorrow's litigation. In contrast, friendships involve a moral and spiritual attachment entirely devoid of ulterior motive. This is what sets friendships apart from virtually any other form of human communion, and it is the reason why very few relationships actually qualify as "friendly."

This last point, Aristotle's insistence on the rarefied essence of friendship, is another proposition contemporary society needs to consider seriously. Increasingly, the line between "friend" and friendly acquaintance has become blurred in our culture. I suspect there are two reasons for this. First, the prevailing habit of mind is generally disinclined to consider such questions. How often can we say we have spent time critically assessing the meaning and content of our relationships? This is not to suggest such a review would be without benefit or significance. It is simply to say that assessments such as these have wrongly been assigned a low priority in the larger economy of modern living.

A second point I suspect has contributed to an incapacity to grasp properly the important qualitative distinctions governing relationships is the role of computerized social networking. There is no question that the computer has done much to foster human exchange on an unprecedented scale. In this regard, it must be seen as one of the most revolutionary forces in the history of human communication. At the same time, however, it must also be acknowledged that electronic correspondence is a poor substitute for direct, face-to-face interaction. Reading a communiqué off a computer screen is no substitute for a handshake or a hug. Nor is it a means by which one can accurately gauge the complexities of human personality. A computer screen provides far too many opportunities to obscure the critical intimations and nuances requisite for a real relationship. In a sense, then, computers have played an ambivalent role with regard to modern human relations. On the one hand, it has brought together people from around the world and fostered a communication system that has greatly advanced the "globalization" of the species. On the other hand, it has simultaneously erected electronic barriers between people. What, in essence, we have done is exchange immediate but limited accessibility for superficial and trivial contacts however unlimited. In so doing, we have greatly complicated the delicate and intricate process by which friendships are forged. We have created an environment rife with opportunity for miscalculating what constitutes a true friendship. A perfect example of all this is the Facebook phenomenon. As of this writing, there are approximately one billion Facebook members worldwide. This remarkable statistic suggests the power of social networking and the attraction it holds for people around the world. The problem, however, with websites such as these lies in their ability to distort the relationships among subscribers. Recently, a young woman in one of my classes boasted to classmates that she had hundreds of "friends" on her Facebook page. Hundreds of friends? I in no way question the integrity of this woman's claim to popularity, but I do challenge her understanding of the word "friend." What computer technology has done is encourage a diluted understanding of a term, which is, by its very nature, defined by exclusivity. To one degree or another, we have all become guilty of rendering "friendship" anemic by a massive over-application of the term. How does one share the same soul with hundreds of people?

As I indicated earlier, one of the best ways to re-establish inter-subjective reality in this matter is to consider the evaluation set forth by Aristotle more than twenty-three hundred years ago. The central premise of his argument is that the commonality of concern and affection that goes into a friendship is a rare and privileged thing. There is nothing casual or superficial about such relationships and they are hardly something one can instantly manufacture by a few strokes on a keyboard. Authentic friendships can only emerge over time, and they only come about when two individuals are prepared to invest significant amounts of emotional and psychological capital selflessly. This has always been an exceedingly uncommon thing, perhaps even more rare today than it was in Aristotle's day, given our culture's predilection for immediate, egoistic indulgence. How many times in life are you likely to discover another human being who is prepared to elevate your interests to a level equal to their own, if not higher? Just think about that for a moment. Now think about the absurdity of anyone claiming to have a phalanx of friends! The only way such an assertion can be made is in light of a preposterously distended understanding of the word "friend."

So, this is what I suggest you need bear in mind regarding the issue of friendship. Recognize from the outset that a true friend is a rare and precious thing. When you establish such a relationship do everything in your power to extend and deepen the bonds that unite you. There are always strains and tensions in any human relation, and friendships are no exception. There will be times when your friend's conduct confuses and disappoints you, but if in fact the person is a true friend, episodes such as these will be short-lived. In the end, nothing and no one can permanently compromise relationships such as these. Genuine friends are quick to forgive and forget because they understand that in the larger scheme of things temporary disenchantments are trivial and unimportant. What is significant are the moments friends share on life's path. There is no better person with whom one can experience the joys and sorrows of this world than a true friend. In happy times, no celebration is complete without their laughter, and in troubled times their heartfelt counsels are essential in making the burdens of life tolerable. Accordingly, the value of good friends is beyond price. They are the sustenance and the savor of life without whom our existence becomes little more than a dreary, pallid, disagreeable assignment. If, then, as an adult you can honestly identify a few individuals as genuine friends in the Aristotelian sense, count yourself blessed. But remember, the number of those so identified is unlikely ever to exceed the digits on one hand.

Efforts to be a Good Christian

Approximately eighty-five percent of Americans identify them-selves as Christians—but what is meant by this designation? How does the typical American "Christian" understand this identity? To what degree do American Christians comprehend their duties and commitments? And, more importantly, to what degree do they operationalize these obligations in their daily lives? I suspect that the vast majority of Christians have little or no real understanding of what their faith entails. More specifically, I believe that most Christians are remarkably ignorant of the rigors demanded of those who profess allegiance to Christ, that they are typically oblivious of the degree to which their life codes fail to comply with even the most rudimentary precepts of their Church. Although I am pre-pared to admit there are indeed a few "real" Christians out there, I am nevertheless convinced that the vast majority of us are at best ersatz Christians, anemic reflections of a religion whose demands for devotion and sacrifice often prove powerfully dissuasive. In the face of its intimidating exhortations it is an easy thing to embrace Christianity's imagery while spurning its substance. While we are often prepared to perform dutifully a ritual Kabuki on Sunday morning, when it comes to allowing the message to penetrate, I mean really penetrate to the core of our being, neither the spirit nor the flesh seems particularly willing. As a result, we may leave the church parking lot with an incipient spiritual glow, but, alas, this peculiar incandescence doesn't last very long. By the time we return home we are back in civilian mode. Our brief stint as soldier of Christ is over, and we will not take up our post again until the following Sunday. In the meantime, we aggressively embrace our secular deployment and do so with such energy and zeal that the experiences of the previous weekend are rendered frail and feeble. So much for lived Faith!

How does one account for these tepid convictions? Of course, there is no simple explanation for any of this, but one component is the secular distractions of modern living. How does one maintain a spiritual disposition in the wake of a society aggressively committed to values and purposes which are almost entirely antithetical? No one should ignore or minimize the undeniable contradictions between what we hear from the pulpit and the instruction offered by the culture at large. On Sundays we are told that charity, forgiveness, and love are the indispensable ingredients of discipleship, that Christians must commit to these other-regarding prescriptions if they are to be numbered among the faithful. On the other six days of the week, however, we are systematically bombarded by a counter-message, conveyed by every conceivable medium, that points in precisely the opposite direction. Here we are told life is a zero-sum contest, that nice guys finish last, that charity extended without prior authorization by a CPA is a sucker's move, and that the meek inherit nothing. As for forgiving our enemies, we are, in essence, urged to endorse the quip of the German poet Heinrich Heine, who said "I always forgive my enemies, but only after they've been hanged." All of this points to a major challenge confronting those who bear the cross. From its inception Christianity has functioned as a counter-cultural voice; this has been its gift and its glory. But today, I fear that voice is increasingly ignored in favor of a profane siren's song that says the vanities of life are all that really matter. These seductive encouragements have served to confuse and complicate religious identity. How does one remain properly devoted to Christian teaching when the golden calf is advanced so compellingly as an alternative? St. Paul once advised that the wisdom of this world is foolishness, but the spirit of our age seeks to invert this famous reproach. It is now God's wisdom that is made to seem foolish.

A second possible explanation for Christian misconception ironically may be the various churches themselves. In recent years, virtually all of the myriad Christian denominations have tended to soften the arduous essence of discipleship, to downplay the self-renunciatory nature of the faith. Consciously or unconsciously, this may have been done in an attempt to facilitate membership, to keep people in the pews for the obvious reason that the irksome demands of this faith are a hard sell in comparison to society's gospel of self-gratification. In any event, many versions of today's Christianity are as much social mechanism as they are churches. In the name of building community, these houses of worship have become catering services, travel bureaus, bingo parlors, and auction houses. Now, please understand, there is nothing wrong with cultivating fellowship. In fact, this can be an important ingredient in advancing the principles and purposes of the faith. There are, however, points beyond which the means become ends and the true Christian telos (end or purpose) is obscured, if not entirely lost in parish social activities. If the only way a church can raise money for itself is to sponsor a cotillion, then it needs to be very concerned with the spiritual disposition of its parishioners. I am not aware of any statements in the apostolic teaching that could possibly justify a cash-and-carry approach to the faith. The fact that many churches are, of necessity, so heavily involved in these subsidiary functions is an unfortunate sign of the times. But most importantly, these activities have served to further deflect our attention from the Church's true vocation. In particular, such activities candy-coat the radical depth of commitment and sacrifice prescribed by Christ. The net effect of all this is a widespread mentality among Christians that their obligations as followers of this religion are fittingly discharged by attending a golf outing. Yet, to the best of my knowledge, Jesus did not own a set of Tour Edge Exotics.

How, then, are we to understand the normative core of Christianity, and by that I mean the irreducible foundations of the faith in the absence of which it loses its relevance and worth as a spiritual instruction? To begin with, it is imperative that you accept the fact that Christianity is not a "feel good faith." When Christ sets forth the conditions of discipleship he specifically says, "Whoever wishes to come after me must deny himself, take up his Cross, and follow me." This was not an invitation to pull-up a chair and get comfortable. He is demanding a sacrificial mentality on your part, one in which the normal pursuits of self-interest are suspended in favor of those less fortunate. In addition, the ominous reference to taking up the cross means exactly what it says. True Christians must be prepared to shoulder the cross-beam and stumble their way toward Golgotha. Just as Christ was spat upon, humiliated, and lashed, you too, in a manner of speaking, must be willing to accept similar treatment. Remember Jesus's words as he commissioned the Twelve: "I am sending you like sheep in the midst of wolves." Be prepared, in other words, for pain and suffering because the world that you must "convert" is a recalcitrant and violent place where those of a generous spirit are routinely ground into dust. This is the stern voice of Christian duty. It summons the would-be Christian to a life of anxiety and grief. So be prepared. The next time you consider your status as a follower of the Son of Man, think crown of thorns, not the most recent church supper.

There is another obstacle to authentic Christian identity beyond the obvious hostilities awaiting those who would minister to the present age. It concerns the spiritual disposition required of a genuine Christian. Unlike most other faiths, Christianity is a supremely inwardly oriented religion. In other words, merely abstaining from certain foods or praying five times a day is not a sufficient expression of one's religious obligations. The mandates of Christian responsibility are never properly discharged by facile gestures of ritual obedience no matter how colorful or entertaining the rituals may be. This is so because the true measure of this faith lies not in pageantry but in the interior disposition of the worshiper. This stress on interiority is a direct inheritance from Judaism which distinguished itself from all other ancient religions by insisting that God was not concerned with burnt offerings nearly as much as he was with pure and compassionate hearts (see the prophetic teachings of Hosea and Isaiah). Christianity extended this logic further, suggesting that even an errant thought might constitute sin (Matt. 5).

The implications of all this should be clear. A real Christian is never off-duty. Even after having fulfilled all of the required liturgical obligations, the follower of Christ has merely scratched the surface in efforts to demonstrate fidelity to the Word. Every hour of every day, the titular Christian must wage an internal war in an effort to achieve and maintain spiritual purity and, it should be understood, every moment of this struggle is presumably scrutinized by the bearer of glad tidings. No machination is conceivable here; it is impossible to mislead or confound divine assessment. God knows every secret, measures every utterance, and gauges the sincerity of every tear. The Bible advises that God even knows the number of hairs upon your head. And so, we are continuously called upon to examine and re-examine the true motives underlying every choice and decision. Thus, no good Christian sleeps well at night! Every Christian is called upon to be a flagellant who continuously scars his own soul. But how many can honestly say they are willing and able to pay such a price?

If there remains any doubt as to the demands of genuine faith, the Bible provides us with a paradigmatic example which is inspirational and intimidating at the same time. I refer to the terrifying experience of the Jewish patriarch Abraham, the man Kierkegaard called "the father of faith." After many years, God finally grants Abraham and Sarah their lifelong wish—a son named Isaac. Needless to say, Isaac is the most precious thing in Abraham's world, a priceless source of joy and hope. But Abraham soon receives instruction from God that the youngster is to be offered up as a holocaust! Imagine the unspeakable anguish of a father ordered by God to slaughter by his own hand the most beloved person in his life? Yet he is prepared to act upon God's instruction because his faith in the Lord's ultimate righteousness is unqualified. Even in the face of this absurd mandate, Abraham remains steadfast and is prepared to engage in a leap of faith that might result in the death of his own child. And so Abraham builds the altar and arranges the wood, but still he believes. He binds the boy's arms and places him on the altar, but still he believes. He takes up the knife and is ready to strike his dear son, but still he believes, and in the end his faith triumphs. The boy is spared, and Abraham is described later as receiving "every blessing" from God.

While the Christian disciple is unlikely to experience anything as tormenting as the Abrahamic crucible, the fundamental message of the biblical story remains relevant for all those who would claim the status of "Knight of Faith." Specifically, you must understand that the path you seek is narrow and steep, that your affiliation with Christ demands that you become a companion in his pain and suffering. Remember that our word for "witness" comes from the ancient word for "martyr" which means your spirit must be prepared to groan just as His did at Gethsemane. In particular, you must be prepared to feel the stings of despair, self-doubt, and isolation on a regular basis. Above all, know this, dangling a cross around your neck or taking a few laps around a rosary is no guarantee of

Christian piety, and the moment you begin to believe it is, you have, in your own self-admiring way, betrayed your Christian calling. Finally, consider the advice offered in Matthew's gospel, "Many are called, but few are chosen." Strive to be worthy of the chosen few if you seek to walk with the Lamb.

Beauty of Another Sort

I have already made clear my views on the importance of the aesthetic in human affairs, as well as my conviction that much of modern art has betrayed its historic mission by renouncing the mystery of beauty. Rather than lend wings to the human spirit, modern art has too often contented itself with narcissistic experiments routinely devoid of cultural merit. But the purpose of this brief chapter is not to reprise my earlier rebuke of modern art. Instead, I wish to describe three major sources of "beauty" and to evaluate each in terms of its capacities to enrich the human experience.

The first, and most obvious category, involves the various species of art we create—painting, poetry, sculpture, music, song and dance. No one should minimize the significance of these pursuits. They are not auxiliary components of civilized life; they are essential features of culture that nourish and extend the spiritual horizon of humanity. In addition, they have the ability to mitigate many of the untoward moments of life. No one can reasonably anticipate immunity from the tears and suffering that inexorably attend human existence. But we are capable of managing a good deal of the pain, and one of our strongest allies in this regard is the beauty we ourselves are capable of creating. This premise was well understood by Nietzsche, who as a young man recognized that beauty was a necessary and fundamental ingredient in our efforts to make this "horrid grind" bearable. In other words, beauty is a kind of salve that we apply to the wounds of life. It grants us, notwithstanding much ugliness and absurdity, the ability to remain positive about the human condition. Indeed, it may be that aesthetic phenomena are the prime means by which we justify existence itself.

The second aesthetic category has a special majesty and splendor far beyond the capacities of human artifice. I refer to the astonishing artistry of Mother Nature. Long before our species came to occupy this planet, Nature had assiduously arranged the details of her palette in ways that resulted in aesthetic magic. Fire, ice, wind, and water were the instruments by which she proclaimed her genius creating in the process natural wonders that humble and exhilarate the human spirit as few experiences can. I offer two illustrations of my point. Many years ago I had an opportunity to stand alone at Cape Sounion and watch the sun slip gently into the Mediterranean. Witnessing this event helped me understand why the ancients selected this particular locale for their temple to the god Poseidon. I suspect they shared exactly the same kind of impressions I had twenty-five hundred years later—this great fiery ball swallowed by Homer's wine dark sea. Not only was the physical appearance of this immersion a spectacular sight to behold, it also brought to mind notions of the eternal rhythms of Nature. I appreciated deeply my great privilege in having observed a solar baptism that had played-out for millions of years before my life began and would continue long after my life was over. In a way, nature's beauty had invited me to participate in one of her most wondrous periodicities—despite my humble status as ephemeral creature. I was, and remain, greatly moved.

The second episode I offer as an illustration of Nature's artistry took place closer to home at one of America's most famous tourist spots, the Grand Canyon. It was early Spring and a close friend and I had made plans to run from rim to rim. We had chosen this time of year in the hope that the weather would still be fairly cool and that we might avoid the crush of visitors typical of the Summer season. In any event, on one fine Saturday morning at 4:30 a.m. my friend and I found ourselves standing at the Bright Angel trailhead facing East waiting for sunrise. As one might imagine, there is a good deal of adrenaline surge in advance of a run like this, so most of our time was spent in nervous chatter and last minute stretching. But when Helios made his mighty appearance, as if on cue, we both fell into a solemn silence. With awe we watched as a magnificent dawn stretched across the canyon, flooding everything with the warm glow of a new day. My friend and I exchanged no words— there was no need to do so. Each understood what the other was experiencing. As the daylight proceeded to pierce the darkness, I recall feeling a certain melancholy on two scores. First an experience like this has a tendency to make one feel very small and very inconsequential. In the larger scheme of things, as demonstrated by this incredible sunrise, it is difficult not to conclude that humanity enjoys about as much significance as a fly-speck. In addition, the timeless quality of what I was observing inevitably forced me to consider the terrible impermanence of all things human. The scenery I was surveying had seen millions of sunrises, but my friend and I, even under the best of circumstances, would only have an opportunity to behold a precious few.

Still, there was another side to this experience, something wonderfully fortifying. Although part of me felt like a superfluous afterthought in Nature's grand economy, at the same time I felt a sense of belonging. Humble status notwithstanding, I understood that I too was a constituent element in the magnificent drama I saw unfolding that morning. I was experiencing what Freud called an "oceanic" moment, a sense of connectedness to the boundless sovereignty of existence. For me, that sunrise was as much a religious encounter as anything I had ever experienced in church. In fact, I would not hesitate to describe this brief interval as "holy" to the extent it disclosed a spiritual message that remains as evocative today as it was thirty years ago. These are the reasons why I count Mother Nature as the second major source of beauty. In essence, I am concurring with a charming insight offered by Henry David Thoreau, who asserted that "Nature is truth." He was right, and perhaps the purest of her truths lies in the beauty of her mountains, her forests, her oceans and her sunrises.

The final category of beauty brings us back to the realm of man. It involves an aesthetic in a more pickwickian sense of the term beauty. Here, we refer to "art" no longer with regard to galleries and museums but in terms of manner, conduct, bearing, demeanor. I refer to the beauty contained in certain human gestures that indicate a gracefulness of human spirit that can only be properly described as aesthetic. In these pages I have often referred to impositions that burden human existence in particular, the dreadful concision that haunts every life. Yet despite all of the challenges and restraints we face as human beings, despite our innumerable incapacities and limitations, we remain capable of engendering a version of beauty that stands alone in terms of loftiness and dignity. Not even the overwhelming aesthetic authority of Mother Nature can match the power of this transient speck when one individual extends oneself to another human being in a spirit of compassion, generosity, kindness, and sympathy. Herein lies a capacity that allows every human being to transcend the limits of their own biological identity and become a spiritual Leonardo, an artist without paint and canvas, but an artist nonetheless.

For the bulk of my life I was largely unaware of this category of beauty. There were a few intimations of something along these lines that did occur to me in my youth but a full recognition of what I am describing did not become clear to me until I was nearly fifty years old. The circumstance under which this took place remains one of the most painful episodes in my life. I refer to the day my mother was diagnosed with terminal liver cancer. After she had undergone a seemingly interminable battery of tests, the family was summoned to a well-known cancer center in Manhattan where we were to meet with a specialist generally acknowledged as the premier expert on my mother's form of the disease. He was an elderly man, well into his seventies but still actively waging his personal war against this particular malignancy. I say "personal" because I later learned that when he was a young man he had lost his wife to the same illness. It seems that this was his motive for dedicating his professional energies to combating the terrible ailment.

In any event, I recall sitting in a very small meeting room where my mother, father, brother, wife and the physician gathered to share the most recent lab results. The doctor sat to my mother's immediate left, not more than a few feet away. After the exchange of a few pleasantries, the doctor turned to my mother and offered these exact words, "Mrs. Soupios, you've been dealt a bad hand." Now that was not the end of his statement, but from that point on his words, at least for me, became nothing more than background noise. I remember thinking, "Mom has just received her death sentence! How could this be?" Was there to be no joyful rescue, no snatching from the jaws of death? How could this grievous verdict be applied to someone as dear to me as my mother?

As I sat there numb, head whirling, out of the corner of my eye I saw a remarkable thing that momentarily lifted me out of the depths of despair that had seized me. As he delivered his dread pronouncement, the doctor reached over and took my mother's hand and squeezed it. Now here was a man who had undoubtedly offered these or similar words to a thousand other patients during the span of his long career, yet there was nothing "clinical" about the way he conducted himself. There was no insensitivity or callousness, no sense that this was just another routine case of terminal illness. This remarkable act of kindness had an interesting effect upon me. As I witnessed the doctor reaching for my mother's hand, I suddenly realized that the tears that had come to my eyes upon learning of her fate had been supplemented by new tears, tears based now on a beautiful human gesture. Even in the grips of this terrible situation, the generosity the doctor was extending my mother made it bearable for me. I thought to myself that while cancer is an ugly, hideous thing, there is still beauty to be found in life and perhaps the most powerful and profound form of beauty is the kind we produce each time we extend ourselves to others in a spirit of common humanity. Nothing in the Prado, the Louvre, or the Hermitage quite measures up to this "aesthetic," nor anything, for that matter, at Yellowstone or Yosemite.

My experiences that day were, to say the least, bittersweet. On the one hand, I learned that I would soon lose the great maternal constant of my life. At the same time, however, I came to understand the beauty of benevolent human gesture. In particular, I observed a doctor who was not only a gifted surgeon, but an artist skilled in the ways and means of generosity. In his simple expression of compassion, my mother's attending physician had created a bit of "art" that spoke volumes about the beauty of what it means to be a human being. He had, in his own way, affirmed the goodness and dignity of our race by assuring a dying woman that he understood and that he cared. I have yet to discover a beauty more sacred or marvelous than this.

The Politician as Type

In 1925 F. Scott Fitzgerald wrote a short story entitled "Rich Boy" in which he offered the now famous observation, "The rich are different than you and me." He might just as easily have added politicians to his list of unconventional types. Politicians, at whatever level within a political system they operate, are not ordinary people. Their attitudes, aspirations, and approaches to human relations tend to constitute a peculiar subset within the species and, as a category, their inclinations routinely are those of the serpent as opposed to the seraph. This may sound a bit harsh, but I assure you my assessment is neither new nor unique. Plato, for example, writes in his *Seventh Epistle*, that he originally planned on entering public life, the traditional career choice for young men of his rank, but he was so appalled by the deplorable intrigues of Athenian politicians that he opted for the life of the mind instead. What this suggests is that politicians have historically displayed a strong preference for extended moral holidays, that conventional standards of propriety and decency fail to resonate with the typical politician. If further evidence for this premise is required, one need only thumb through the pages of Niccolo Machiavelli's *Prince*, the work Bertrand Russell referred to as a handbook for gangsters. There is lots of juicy reading in this little volume, but the quiddity of his message is contained in chapter 18, where Machiavelli outlines Realpolitik as no one had ever quite done before. Here he argues that in order to enjoy political success, a prince must jettison every moral constraint including the full complement of Christian virtues. Specifically the prince must learn not to keep faith, to prize prudence above principle, to cultivate the art of false appearances, and to conduct himself with the cunning of a fox and the ferocity of a lion (a direct swipe at Cicero's teaching in *De Officiis*). Now, interpreting Machiavelli is no easy matter and there is plenty of scholarly debate about what exactly he intended in the pages of this book, but this much can be said; whether the formulas contained in *The Prince* were intended as genuinely normative or were meant as antimonarchical satire, no author in the Western political tradition has more effectively summarized the mindset and methodology of the political type. While no politician wishes to be labeled with the adjectival form of "Old Nick's" name ("Machiavellian"), to one degree or another they all seem to follow the Florentine's script with unswerving fidelity.

Why is this so? Why do the vast majority of politicians appear to constitute a homogenous grouping along Machiavellian lines? I believe a proper answer to this question can only be found by approaching the issue from a psychological perspective. In other words, there may be certain psychological needs that politicians are attempting to address in their efforts to achieve office. I can offer two examples, both of which relate to the all-important category of power. Clearly, there are some men and women who seem absolutely driven in their quest to secure title and command. These individuals are by no means unique to the political domain; they can be found in a wide variety of venues including the business world and academe. On the surface, they often portray themselves as high-minded and affable, but beneath the surface there lurks an impenitent ruthlessness which routinely renders mute the voice of conscience. Prevarication, machination, and duplicity are coins of the realm for these people. They can operate comfortably along these lines because they have developed an uncanny ability to rationalize and justify any and all chicanery. In short, these individuals represent some of the purest illustrations of what is called "situational ethics." They are quite literally capable of manufacturing moral justifications as circumstances dictate, all with an eye firmly focused on self-interest. This moral minimalism explains the frequency with which betrayals and treacheries are accompanied by exculpatory refrains like "nothing personal." Here, the political type does nothing more than compound deceit with the sin of hypocrisy revealing in the process that the counsels of conscience count for naught to such individuals. But what could possibly impel a person along such a morally bankrupt path?

I believe one possible explanation lies in a distended ego state whose origins may stretch back to childhood. The manner and bearing of many politicians suggest to me an egregiously misguided sense of entitlement. After years of indulgence, years of being told that they merit special acknowledgement and treatment, a good number of those described here as political types, come to believe they do not merely qualify for high office—they deserve it. For these egotistical men and women, entry into public life has nothing to do with civic contribution or concern for the common good. Rather, the egoistic political type views office seeking as little more than a version of personal irredentism, a means by which office is bestowed or returned to its rightful owner. If any of this is remotely accurate, then two additional conclusions follow. First, no one should be the least bit surprised by the galloping ambitions of such individuals. Given the fact that these people believe they are due the political spotlight, it follows that they will engage in just about any behavior to reach their objectives. For them, there are no rules for attaining office, no limits, moral or otherwise. In addition, given the psychological disposition of these vain upstarts, it may be reasonable to assume a certain contempt for those they are sworn to serve. Political narcissists are predictably ill-disposed toward keeping faith with the "people." The people exist to serve their interests, not the other way around. They think sheep ripe for shearing.

The second category of an official who seeks power as a means of fulfilling certain psychological needs is far more nefarious than the simple egoist I've just described. Whereas the first group is clearly comprised of self-absorbed rascals, now we encounter a much smaller and much more perverse category of politician. These are the people who are pathologically impelled by the *libido dominandi*. Again, the motives here are psychological, but in this case ego takes a backseat to fear and hatred. The governing dynamic for these malignant souls is, above all, an all-pervasive sense of insecurity. In this context, the accumulation of power is the sole means by which one comes to feel safe and secure. For some, pathological fears can only be addressed if the environment in which one lives is controlled down to the last detail and this requires that the domineering politician possess unlimited amounts of power. Everyone has encountered this type of personality somewhere along the line, most likely at work. Have you ever been supervised by a "control freak" manager who finds it absolutely impossible to delegate authority honestly to a subordinate and who constantly second guesses the decisions and activities of everyone supervised? Always remember, the instinct to micromanage is not a reflection of lofty work ethic, it is a neurotic symptom of an insecure personality. When this sort of thing happens on the job, the results are typically organizational dysfunction, but when this type of personality attains high office, the results can be apocalyptic. The two great iconic murderers of the 20th century were Adolf Hitler and Josef Stalin, and despite their ideological differences (Fascism v. Marxism), they were, psychologically speaking, identical twins. Both men suffered the effects of violently abusive fathers who instilled in them an all-consuming sense of insecurity. Historical events would suggest these fears were never "outgrown" but remained an excessive and increasingly irrational aspect of their adult lives. This explains why their demands for power were unconditional, why all who stood in their path were eliminated (e.g. Ernst Roehm and Sergei Kirov) and why any group perceived to be unwilling to submit to their absolute control became an object of paranoid loathing. Let's be very clear about the implications of what I have just suggested. Based on the global nightmare unleashed by these monstrous men, there is one apothegm the world can ill-afford to forget, viz., civilized existence itself is menaced every time pathologically insecure individuals are invested with real power. This, because power is a voracious thing. In the wrong hands, it has the capacity to devour everything including reason, justice, and basic human decency.

Thankfully, America has been blessed in the sense that we have never, to date, had to contend with malignant political personalities of this sort. Our challenge does not seem to lie in denying high office to a Hitler as much as it does in fending-off a plague of self-obsessed mountebanks and charlatans. What can we do to protect ourselves against the pettifoggery and sophistry of these people? For one thing we can do a better job in assessing those we put in office. It's very easy to point the finger at unethical politicians as the cause of our economic and social difficulties, but in the final analysis much of the responsibility lies with "the people." H.L. Mencken offered many indelicate references on this point, not the least of which was his colorful taxonomy for the American voter— "boobus Americanus." As a whole, the American people merit a grade of "F" when it comes to doing their political homework. To an amazing degree, they are continuously victimized by the humbug and mummery of candidates because they simply refuse to invest the necessary time scrutinizing the claims and backgrounds of office seekers. Now in fairness to the American voter, modern life is both fast-paced and complicated—who has time to research the credentials of politicians meticulously? People are too busy just trying to earn a living. All of this is true, but it is also true that by abdicating our obligations to be properly informed members of the electorate, we allow political quackery to triumph. In the absence of well-documented political assessments, we rely instead upon what Francis Bacon referred to as the Idols of the Mind. To one degree or another, the American voter is dangerously reliant upon each of the four Idols described by Bacon in his *Novum Organum*—Idols of the Tribe, Idols of the Cave, Idols of the Marketplace, Idols of the Theatre. This is to say, the modern political arena is rife with opportunity for error, misconception, and speciousness all aided and abetted by the commercially driven knavery of certain modern mass media.

What then are we to conclude from all this? First, political harlotry is nothing new. None of this is the least bit unique to 21st century America. The political "types" I have described have always been with us and probably always will be. I am reminded of this every time I read Thucydides and what he has to say about the outrageous political four-flushers depicted in his *History*, such as Cleon and Hyperbolus. Second, we have every right to be suspicious, if not a bit cynical, whenever we consider the integrity of those seeking political office. This is not to say there are no men and women out there who earnestly wish to offer public benefaction. However, please understand instances of true public servants are as rare as hen's teeth. And the higher up in the political system one goes, the more scant these exceptions seem to become. Third, recognize that those who fervently seek public office are not your average people. In most instances, these men and women tend to see life differently than the rest of us. More specifically, their devotion to expediency tends to distinguish them from the majority in ways that place them well beyond the moral mainstream. In light of this, the people cannot realistically insist upon some Edenic innocence on the part of their representatives. At the same time, however, the people have every right to insist on something better than the Whore of Babylon.

This brings me to a final word on the matter of public accountability. When, on rare occasion, a politician is unequivocally linked to some transgressive act the culprit inevitably calls for a press conference. Yet, even here, at this ritualized drama where the betrayer of public trust is supposed to finally come clean, politicians typically remain disingenuous. Instead of earnest contrition, we are merely told the official accepts "full responsibility" for his or her actions. But what is the significance of a confession devoid of consequence? What good is a *mea culpa* in the absence of a resignation? Incessant hypocrisy such as this makes me think the ancient Romans may have had the right idea in the treatment of serious wrongdoers. The malefactor was sewn into a sack with a dog, an ape, a viper, and a rooster and then tossed into the Tiber. How deep is the Potomac?

Lucre—Filthy and Otherwise

The word "lucre" comes from the Latin term *lucrum*, meaning avarice. We sometimes hear the phrase "filthy lucre," which refers to money secured in some shameful manner. The expression was first used by William Tyndale in his translation of the New Testament (see *Titus* 1.7 & 11), and it reflects a long tradition, both biblical and philosophical, that money is often a source of moral and spiritual corruption. What are we to make of these enduring impeachments of money and those who feverishly seek it? This question enjoys a special significance for contemporary society, given the modern fascination with all things financial and the pervasive tendency to assign value in almost exclusively economic terms. Unfortunately, it is precisely this same ardent enthusiasm for wealth that precludes critical assessment, that makes it very difficult to apprehend the positive and negative roles money plays in our culture. We need to take a look at all this in some detail.

Historically speaking, I believe money has gotten a bad rap. Now please understand, I am not suggesting that the many cautionary injunctions about money's capacities to distort and defile human priority are wrong. The record of human history is fraught with examples of depraved acts committed by those for whom money is the alpha and omega of life. What I am proposing is that money per se is not the cause for any of this. Money does not possess some innate capacity to mesmerize and seduce the human spirit. Surely when treachery and deceit do occur, it cannot be attributed to some alchemic potency embedded in our currency notes. The fault lies within us, not the U.S. Treasury Department. More precisely, the errant quest for, and use of money is a symptom of a misguided understanding of the proper role money should play in peoples' lives. Specifically, it reflects a deficient grasp of the critical distinction between means and ends. Money is an important and necessary aspect of a well-lived life, but its value is ultimately instrumental, not intrinsic. In other words, money is "good" in the sense that it can help us attain higher, more important things. It is to be valued as a mechanism that points beyond itself, as a means of securing qualitatively superior fulfillments that stand beyond economic calculation. Those who feverishly commit themselves to the procurement of wealth, who make money the sovereign impulse of their lives, have lost sight of this very important distinction. One of the consequences of such myopia is often an existence in which people live to work rather than work to live—a Faustian bargain.

None of what I have just written escaped the adroit scrutiny of Aristotle, and I recommend him as an invaluable resource whenever your priorities become indistinct or confused. With specific regard to money, I encourage you to consider Aristotle's discussion of "liberality" in bk4 of the *Nicomachean Ethics*. In this context, the reference to "liberal" is not a designation of political preference but rather an attitude toward the acquisition and distribution of wealth. To be "liberal" in antiquity meant you understood the proper way in which wealth was to be employed, and by the term "proper" Aristotle meant virtuous. In other words, the liberal person was an individual committed to doing noble things with his financial resources. He was not concerned with the massive acquisition of wealth as an end in itself but as a potential means of promoting socially estimable acts. This dedication to larger social purpose is so extensive among liberal people that it is almost impossible for them to remain rich. Nevertheless, the distribution of personal financial resources remains a source of pleasure for the liberal man or woman—even though this sense of joy may make one vulnerable to the fiscal rascality of less scrupulous individuals.

By modern standards, Aristotle's understanding of liberality is at best "quaint" and at worst a disastrously unrealistic approach to financial management. In the "real" world, meaning by that the cutthroat environment of the marketplace, there is little room for liberality. Here, the twin gods of avarice and cupidity reign supreme with the result that concerns for virtue and nobility constitute the royal road to chapter 11. But before we dismiss the ancient logic out of hand, let's consider a few points. First, there is some truth to the idea that money is a necessary ingredient in the good life. But, in and of itself, money is not sufficient for the good life. For are there not a variety of very important human experiences that are beyond the capacity of money to guarantee such as love, health, friendship? Second, we need to ask what is meant by phrases such as "the good life." Aristotle may have had a clearer understanding of what this means because he appreciated the instrumental nature of money. This allowed him to avoid the kind of obfuscating conclusions that result from inverting means and ends. In short, it may be that Aristotle was able to prioritize human aspirations in ways that we find almost impossible to replicate today. Whereas he was capable of raising the all-important teleological question (i.e., What is the ultimate life objective for a human being?), today we seem incapable of even formulating such a question, much less providing a well-reasoned answer. Mired as we are in the logic of Dun & Bradstreet, how can there be a goal, purpose, or objective higher than a well-fed wallet? Aristotle believed the *telos*, or end of human endeavor, was the fulfillment of our rational and moral potentials. In comparison to this ideal, doesn't modern material aspiration bear the stench of compromise, the fetid aroma of lowest common denominator?

This last point raises the important issue of consequences. What is the likely consequence for a society where the sole value, the sole good, the sole aspiration is conceived in economic terms? I can summarize the impact in one word, "distortion." By its very nature, a culture in which money is the supreme value will suffer the effects of systematic misconception in virtually every compartment of life. In this regard, I am reminded of a memorable quip about how it is possible to know the price of everything and the value of nothing (Oscar Wilde). Value assessments require a point of reference, an ultimate standard by which value differences can be perceived and formulated. If, however, there is no notion of axiological "end," no measure by which to draw qualitative distinctions, mere instrumentalities are afforded the opportunity to masquerade as objects of ultimate worth. Any civilization that hopes to advance the cause of human culture in the absence of clear and sound distinctions of value is doomed to failure. It will succeed only in advancing the mundane, the trite, the nihilistically trivial. Even worse, it will prove incapable of diagnosing its own deficiencies. Nothing more powerfully distorts reality than a gilded cage.

Another distortive effect of allowing money to function as the all-comprehensive value of society involves social dynamics, how we understand each other as human beings. Here, I offer a famous moral precept advocated by Immanuel Kant, who said, "Always treat people as ends in themselves, never as a means to an end." But is loyalty to this principle conceivable in a society where nearly everyone is prepared to offer an all-abasing obeisance at the altar of mammon? In environments where the instinct for commodification is strong everything is assigned its "price" and, unfortunately, that includes human qualities and even human beings themselves. Stop and consider this for a moment. A woman's beauty, an athlete's strength, an inventor's creation— all are viewed as commodities; all are assessed and measured from a financial perspective and assigned a monetary value. Human qualities tend to get misplaced in a process such as this, and, as a result, people tend to be correspondingly de-valued. A person's worth is necessarily seen in terms of potential as a revenue generating entity. There is a peculiar wrong in all this which Karl Marx correctly understood. Commodities don't just fall from the sky. They are created by people to enhance the material condition of humankind. Over time, however, commodities can become objects of fetishistic attachment; i.e. under certain conditions they can take on a mysterious life of their own, at least in the confused imaginations of some people, just as the idols created by primitive man were worshipped as gods. In the end, people subordinate themselves to the very things they create and, in the process, further distort both their own identities and the identities of others. I suspect this is what Emerson meant when he complained that "things are in the saddle and ride mankind." The point is that none of this can happen unless a society has become perversely engrossed in financial considerations. It is impossible to view this sort of disproportion as indicative of societal health—massive GDP notwithstanding.

Perhaps the most disturbing way in which a confused understanding of money can distort human perspective is its ability to corrupt fair and honest assessment. When it comes to justifying financial self-interest, apparently there is a limitless human capacity to manipulate, distort, and even invent the truth. Here, it seems, objectivity and fair-mindedness don't stand a chance. Under these circumstances truth becomes a kind of putty that is stretched and pulled in any direction economic advantage might dictate. In the end, the impact of all this can seriously jeopardize the long-term well-being of a culture because the exegetical integrity of almost everything is rendered suspect. No text, no news report, no website can be trusted to convey information in a "fair and balanced" manner, i.e. without undue concern for market share and sales revenues. I am afraid even historical literature is vulnerable to this kind of financially motivated skewing. Take, for example, Adam Smith's seminal tome *The Wealth of Nations*. No one can legitimately question this famous treatise's status as the "Bible" of free-market economics. What we can question, however, is the selective use of this famous text as the mystical grimoire of capitalism. In an effort to promote their financial metaphysic, the free market hierophants have presented a thoroughly *ex parte* interpretation of *The Wealth of Nations*. Specifically, they have sought to invest the productive energies of self-interest with a moral justification which, in truth, reflects a position contrary to Smith's actual views. In great measure, these distorted perspectives have gained credibility because the modern champions of laissez-faire have conveniently neglected to consider the other book Smith wrote entitled *The Theory of Moral Sentiments*. Smith's work on political economy was actually intended as a continuation of this earlier moral treatise. No effort to understand Smith's message fully and accurately can afford to ignore this nexus, but, of course, this is exactly what has occurred. As a result, we have been led to believe that market dynamics are the whole of life, that the unbridled accumulation of wealth is an unqualified good; and that the best way to serve the larger good is to ignore the larger good (i.e. to believe private vice, by some legerdemain, conduces to public virtue). The degree to which these ideas simplistically and self-servingly misrepresent the logic of Adam Smith is well demonstrated by the following passage from *The Wealth of Nations*

> The wise and virtuous man is at all times willing that his own private interest should be sacrificed to the public interest of his own particular order of society—that the interests of this order of society be sacrificed to the greater interest of the state. He should therefore be equally willing that all those inferior interests should be sacrificed to the greater interest of the universe, to the interests of that great society of all sensible and intelligible beings, of which God himself is the immediate administrator and director (bk 5 ch. 1, part 3).

What Smith is advancing here is the Stoic notion of a moral cosmos which includes a series of ethical and social incumbencies upon all rational beings, including the shopkeeper, the merchant, and the banker. Doesn't sound very much like Ayn Rand, does it? Indeed, it is difficult to imagine a position more distant from the slash and burn mentality of modern capitalism. Yet the words and images of Adam Smith are routinely invoked to justify economic values and approaches that Smith himself found morally impermissible.

Now, let's attempt to put this all into perspective. First, none of what I have written here is intended to encourage an ascetic lifestyle. I see no particular value in wearing a hair shirt and eating wild honey. We live in a time of remarkable prosperity, and there is nothing inherently wrong with a reasonable involvement in the bounty of modern life. Indeed, I fully agree the life worth living requires that we concern ourselves to some degree with financial factors. However, we need to guard against a powerfully reductionist logic in our culture that judges everything by a monetary standard. Against this measure, no principle, no cause, no value is deemed worthy except to the extent it contributes to financial advantage. It is specifically under the terms of this reasoning that lucre has the potential of becoming "filthy." Here, I am reminded of a term Plato employs disparagingly in the early sections of his *Republic*. The word is *pleonexia*, which refers to disproportion in the sense of demanding more than one's fair share. Plato conceives of this, first and foremost, as a psychological disorder, but since society is simply the individual written large, he is quick to point out the larger social and political consequences of a malady such as this. Viewed through a Platonic lens, it is difficult to avoid the conclusion that our society does a good deal more than simply tolerate pleonexia. When it comes to money it has embraced it as a fundamental cultural premise. Endorsement such as this not only encourages moral memory loss, it also obfuscates larger human potential—a necessary consequence of promoting the belief that human destiny extends no further than the nearest ATM machine.

These confusions are advanced further by a variety of economic partisans who revile any who dare challenge the prevailing dogma that financial self-interest is the only good. There are two means by which these advocates of the almighty buck seek to discredit their opponents. First, they attempt to commandeer the narrative by attributing new and defamatory meanings to words suggestive of alternative viewpoints. In their hands, for example, words like "charity" and "altruism" are re-coded to suggest a perverse and irrational sacrifice of legitimate self-interest. In some respects, this form of lexical manipulations is disturbingly reminiscent of Orwell's Ministry of Truth where "war is peace, freedom is slavery, and ignorance is strength." The second tactic employed by advocates of the financial imperative entails a virtual consecration of the capitalist system. Here free enterprise is endowed with something approaching divine sanction. Whereas previous economic models were merely historical, for modern advocates capitalism enjoys a transhistorical superiority bordering on the mystical. This explains the peculiar rhetoric routinely invoked by defenders of the free market who would have us believe the Holy Spirit is prepared to dwell therein but only if government regulation is kept to a minimum. Such an argument is used to advance the notion that those who fail to support the economic credo of capitalism are not simply unAmerican; they are also in some larger sense repugnant to all that is holy and righteous. God bless the Chicago School of Economics!

What, then, should be your position on the proper role of money in life? First off, as in everything else, make sure your position is a carefully considered one. In this context, that means you must avoid the logic of both the ideologue and the self-regarding cynic. The former, because groundless conviction rarely results in legitimate insight, and the latter, because few things more readily misdirect heart and mind than economic self-interest. Instead, remind yourself that money is neither intrinsically good nor intrinsically evil. Whatever virtue it may possess lies in what you do with it. If you use it to advance larger, responsible purposes then you can be counted among those who have learned an essential life lesson. If, on the other hand, you allow money to become an all-consuming concern, if you allow it to own you and to determine who and what you are as a person, you have abdicated your birthright as a rational creature. More specifically, you have enfranchised means at the expense of ends and, in the process, rendered yourself a candidate for moral and spiritual bankruptcy. Rather than live life along these lines, recognize the real value of financial resource lies in its ability to facilitate the highest potential of a human being. Ask yourself how you might "give birth to a dancing star" as Nietzsche says, as opposed to obsessing over your money market account. Do not forget that living well is an art that surely requires financial resource but that, above all, it demands understanding, perspective and a sense of priority. Let not the worm of mammon poison your being.

Personhood

The word "personhood" can have a variety of meanings and applications. Today, the term has become heavily embroiled in the abortion debate, specifically, as part of the contentious question of when an embryo is to be recognized as a human being. Several religious groups have argued that personhood begins the instant sperm penetrates ovum. Many ethicists have argued, however, that this reasoning is a reflection of religious dogma, not the result of unencumbered philosophic reflection. Fortunately, this nettlesome issue does not concern us because my reference to "personhood" has nothing to do with *in vivo* identifications. What I wish to discuss instead is the idea of a developmental sequence that needs to occur in every human life. In particular, I wish to argue against any notion that human personhood is a precise and finite thing, that there is some climactic moment when our efforts in this regard reach a state of complete fruition. In short, on this particular question I find myself drawn irresistibly in the direction of an ancient philosopher named Heraclitus, who said *panta rhei* —all things are in flux. My point is, we too are subject to that great vortex of change to which the ancient thinker referred. The only question is by what means will we be shaped and reshaped. Will we be formed by self-determined strategies, or will we be forged by poorly understood and blindly conceived cultural forces?

I believe there are some very good reasons for investigating this sort of issue, given the prevalence of a certain misconception. The misguided view goes something like this: Personhood is a status everyone enjoys automatically. It is an innate aspect of human existence, an ontological state we legitimately claim the moment we enter this life. I have an idea a good portion of this logic is traceable to the natural rights doctrine promoted during the Enlightenment Era. In an effort to advance the notion of certain inalienable political guarantees, a teaching arose that all men were endowed with a fundamental core of rights beyond legitimate revocation or infringement. None of these rights required that an individual engage in any particular mode of conduct. In short, these were not privileges one had to earn, they were quite literally endowments granted at the moment of birth. It is from these foundations that a distorted idea of personhood may have arisen. In the same way one does not have to lift a finger to enjoy natural rights, there is little or no effort required to achieve the status of "person." By dint of an obstetric act alone, we arrive at some ripened condition as a human being. This is the assumption I find not only wrongheaded, but to some degree, dangerous in the sense that it speciously relieves of us certain burdens requisite for proper human identity.

Now there is, of course, a sense in which birth alone does grant personhood, i.e., physical identity, and were we protozoan creatures there would be no further need for discussion. But it is precisely because we are not merely physical entities that a host of other, very complex questions arise regarding human personhood. By our very nature we must concern ourselves with issues of intellectual, social, moral, and spiritual progress. Any theory, philosophy, or cultural setting that denies these uniquely human responsibilities is not only misrepresenting what it means to flourish as a human being, it may also be guilty of empowering injurious forces, forces that are less committed to the realization of unique human capacities and more concerned to promote mindless activities resulting in a pseudo-personhood born of default. What I am suggesting is that attaining the status of genuine personhood is a process that demands concerted effort on the part of the individual. Among other things, it necessitates a clear understanding that cultural forces can have a mummifying effect upon human potential. In particular, they are capable of encouraging a kind of abdication of responsibility by offering a less arduous path than the rigorous road required of robust personhood. In short, we need to be aware of how compellingly society can compromise both perspective and aspiration by advancing bovine contentment as a life strategy. Unfortunately, too much of modern culture's message would have us believe that the fully evolved human being is little more than a dutiful consumer, that material accoutrement is somehow synonymous with the achievement of human personality. I believe this is a parlous mentality in at least two respects. First, there is an obvious tendency here to reduce human possibility to the lowest common denominator. Abraham Maslow famously presented a scheme he called the Hierarchy of Needs where the full-range of human capacities were presented as a pyramidal structure. The base of the pyramid represented rudimentary biological needs while the upper levels of the structure presented the more elevated potentials human beings possess. I believe a strong case can be made for the idea that modern society is too quick to ignore the apex of this pyramid, that we are bombarded with message and imagery that exhorts pursuing the lower segments of Maslow's edifice to the near exclusion of everything else. Instead of being told we must reach for the heights, we are counseled to seek no satisfactions beyond an increasingly superfluous array of creature comforts. We are, it would seem, advised to forsake the sublime in favor of the prosaic. The implications of all this are all too clear with regard to fulfilling the potentials inherent in human identity.

In addition to numbing us to who and what we should be striving to become, in matters such as these culture also has the power to seduce. By encouraging a diluted notion of human potential, society provides a rationale for not engaging in the hard work of becoming a person. If all that is involved in achieving human potential is a comfortable lifestyle, why bother engaging in the restless, painful quest for self? Why not just sit back and allow a stream of random cultural forces to flow over us, to shape us, to determine our fate? In other words, we are lured into thinking that there is no significant consequence attached to abdicating our potential for inner-directedness, that an all-encompassing heteronomy is just fine. But the truth is it is not fine and it is not fine for either the individual or society. No culture that tolerates the production of partially actualized human beings can hope to amass the spiritual resources requisite for its own health and well-being, perhaps not even for its own survival. In the end, a civilization is only as good as the human capital it produces. If society endorses a notion of human possibility that devalues who and what people are capable of becoming, and if it is prepared to allow these diminished norms to serve as the guiding precepts of culture, clearly, the course that lies ahead is fraught with difficulty. Where, and how, amid such uninspiring arrangements, do we arrive at critical reflection, creative insight, and exalted aspiration?

I believe the "where" is easy to identify, viz., the properly evolved human person. The "how" is a far more complicated matter, not only because society tends to favor languid throngs as opposed to masses of discerning men and women, but because individuals themselves often shrink from the rigors of self-cultivation. Separating oneself from the unaspiring mass is a progenitive act and, like any process of giving birth, it involves anxiety and pain. The first instinct of those challenged with the demands of personhood is to remain blissfully embedded in the herd. There is a good reason for this. What we are considering here is a process in which people quite literally reinvent themselves on a continuous basis. This is no easy task given the fact that it requires a remarkable capacity for candid self-assessment and here is where most people begin to falter. Why? Because there is no more difficult, no more intimidating task than a ruthlessly candid examination of self. To go down deep inside, to sweep aside the excuses and the blame shifting to mercilessly deny yourself any clemency with regard to personal responsibility, this is the price that must be paid on behalf of genuine personhood and it is a price few are able or willing to pay. In the face of such an intimidating mandate, people routinely construct massively fraudulent justifications for themselves. Indeed, it seems we are able to endure only very small amounts of reality when it comes to honest self-appraisal, with the result that we are all fully capable of manufacturing our own truths. The difficulty in all this is obvious—where personal assessment is fettered by analytic deceit and psychological cowardice, there is little or no prospect for the achievement of personhood. You must gird your loins, my friend, and be prepared for much disconcertion, disillusionment, and discomfort—the inescapable coins of this realm.

How does one prepare for such a daunting mission? Begin by viewing your life as a continuous project. Accept the premise that you are a provisional and imperfect creature whose job in life is to seek a progressively higher and better state of being. By your very nature, you enjoy these possibilities, but, at the same time, you are also strongly inclined to surrender your potentials because the freedom implied by your conditional state includes the intimidating burden of responsibility. Perhaps the best way to shoulder this oppressive weight is to dedicate yourself to a life governed by earnestly conceived principles. This may sound pretty obvious. Who isn't governed by some system of principles? Upon closer examination, however, we discover that the directing "principles" that tend to guide most peoples' lives are not all that principled. In other words, I reject the commonly held view that the spirited pursuit of self-interest constitutes a formula conducive to the development of legitimate personhood. Those who dedicate themselves along these lines cannot be said to possess anything approximating a meaningful set of standards. Instead, their lives are commanded by a moral fluidity that says personal conduct is an entirely protean affair, a series of self-regarding exercises dictated by circumstance. In the end, one cannot avoid the conclusion that individuals such as these stand for nothing and that their substance as human beings is as vacuous as the ethical opportunism they advocate. Their values and approaches to life suggest that they have conveniently avoided the merciless audit of self I mentioned earlier, with the result that their lives are stained with *mauvaise fois*—bad faith. And so, in the absence of a legitimate moral center, these individuals are continuously poised on the balls of their feet waiting to pounce on whatever self-indulgent opportunity presents itself. In short, their lives are situationally driven, they are "owned" by what Kant called "empirical considerations," meaning "principled" has no possible application here. It also means we are compelled to ask, how can healthy human identity emerge from a model of conduct such as this?

Needless to say, the more convenient one's moral standard, the more likely it will prove preclusive of personhood as we have used the term. The antidote for much of this lies in the creation of a legitimate life code capable of serving as a "living" behavioral norm. This is accomplished by embracing that crucible of cross-examination that we all, to one degree or another, dread. There is, perhaps, an axiom we can propose here relating to this process: the more fiercely we engage in these lustrations, the more viable the code and the greater our prospects of accomplishing genuine human identity. This all sounds rather neat and readily attainable when laid out as if it were a kind of formula but, of course, nothing could be further from the truth. The cost of personhood is extraordinarily high to the extent it requires us to indentify candidly and to restrain personal interest while simultaneously dispelling our love of self-serving fabrications.

Whenever I consider life lived by code versus life lived by vain reflex my thoughts irresistibly turn to the wonderful biographical comparisons offered by the ancient essayist Plutarch in his *Parallel Lives*. In particular, it is difficult not to juxtapose the exemplary code of Aristides with the abject roguery of Alcibiades. The difference between these two Athenians could not be more stark, nor could their contrasting approaches to life better illustrate the difference between an existence informed by code and one driven by an unbridled sense of self. As it so happens, Alcibiades was a man of enormous talent and personal charm. Had his gifts of leadership been consistently deployed in favor of his native city, as both Plutarch and Thucydides clearly suggest, the outcome of the Peloponnesian War might have been very different. Unfortunately for Athens, Alcibiades was a moral chameleon (Plutarch specifically describes him as such) capable of sloughing moral duty at the slightest hint of personal advantage. The result was disaster, both for this prince of intrigues and for his city-state.

The antithesis of Alcibiades's moral ductility is found in the person of Aristides, a man upon whom the Greeks bestowed the honorific cognomen "The Just." In case after case, Aristides is portrayed as maintaining his worth and dignity as an upright and dutiful human being. In particular, he never allowed expediency to obscure the dictates of justice. Even when he had ample opportunity to inflict harm upon his enemies or to enrich himself at public expense, he consistently refused to betray his moral ideals. There was a price for all this. Indigence was a constant companion throughout his life and we are even told he was incapable of providing dowries for his daughters. Yet, these very real hardships never became a pretext for compromising either his principles or his good name. Plutarch's message is clear: Aristides's modesty of circumstance was more than matched by the glory of his personhood.

So, take these as your two options. One path is slick and narcissistically convenient. It allows for massive rationalization in the face of moral challenge by offering "self" as the only standard by which such questions are to be judged. The result is an "Alcibidian" personality, a moral solipsist who views others as mere means to his ends. In not having engaged in the hard work of critical self-reflection, terms such as "integrity," "honor," and "decency," are meaningless for such an individual. Worse, they tend to be derisively dismissed as the kind of quixotry advanced by dupes and suckers who routinely misconstrue the pragmatic imperatives of life.

In opposition to all this, we have the model offered by Aristides. By every indication, this was a man who lived a life committed to what the Germans call *Vornehmheit*, human nobility. Notwithstanding the many opportunities for fraud and deception we tend to offer ourselves, Aristides apparently achieved a life code in which concern for self included a generous and committed engagement with the larger good. This is the paradigm I offer in terms of genuine personhood. It involves a binding set of principles honestly arrived at, that completely transcend the seductions of prudential calculation. Within such individuals there lies a purity and rigor of will that the majority of people will never experience or even understand, yet it is precisely this sort of will that bestows some of the highest and most enriching moments of life. So please do not be misled by the dazzle and bluster that the Alcibiades of this world will offer you as the proper path. Instead, tread the road set down by Aristidian virtue, a path of quiet heroism guided by principle. And when people mock and deride you as an ingenuous assailant of windmills, remember the words of Anatole France who said, "Without dreamers, mankind would still be living in caves." And finally, be assured that by living your life in the manner I advance here, you will find a special comfort and repose known only to those who have arrived at that rarified identity called "personhood."

Wisdom

In recent years, various members of the scientific community have supplied us with some interesting chronological data. According to cosmologists, for example, the so-called Big-Bang occurred 13.7 billion years ago. By comparison, our planet is a mere infant at only 4.5 billion years of age. Animal life seems to have first appeared on Earth about 550 million years ago in the form of comb jellies, a kind of primitive jellyfish. By comparison with these data, the appearance of Homo sapiens is a truly recent event. Paleoanthropologists suggest modern humans have only been around for about 200,000 years —the blink of an eye in the larger scheme of things. Yet in this incredibly brief period of time our species has come to dominate the planet, along with many of the forces we associate with the term "nature." By way of illustration, consider this: Somewhere about 10,000 years ago in Mesopotamia, man first invented the wheel. Just think of what we have achieved since the development of this early technological breakthrough. Think of computers, the medical sciences, telecommunications and remind yourself of the astounding rapidity with which humanity has registered these achievements. Recall that the Wright brothers famously defied gravity in December 1903 for a grand total of 12 seconds and a flight distance of 120 feet. Sixty-six years later, Neil Armstrong stood on the moon!

What does this say about our species and its ability to solve problems and, specifically, to convert wild fantasy into concrete reality? Obviously it says a great deal indeed. The record of human accomplishments may at first seem to corroborate Goethe's description of man in *Faust*, where he is called "Earth's little god." We must remain mindful, however, as Goethe surely was, that despite our many wondrous achievements, we have yet to earn the right of anything approximating divine status. For all of our many scientific and technological successes, there remain certain obstacles and deficiencies that stubbornly resist remedy. As a category, these long-standing impediments to improvement have less to do with the physical environment than they do with our own inner-life. Here, we are not speaking of some incapacity to comprehend the laws of physics, rather, I refer to an inability to comprehend ourselves. Unfortunately, the record of human history unequivocally suggests there has been little or no correlative progress between our command of the physical realm and our control of the malignant forces that continue to torment human affairs. Take, for example, the catastrophic events of the Second World War, where humanity not only demonstrated its continued willingness to convert pruning hooks into spears, it also revealed an unrepentant blood lust that can only be described as "pathological." Tragically, none of this was forestalled by our universities, our cultural triumphs, our technological victories. It would seem none of these things are adequate to the task of subduing the human heart's darkness. Indeed, there is even evidence to suggest progress in these areas often functions as the willing associate of human perversity. Thus, for example, advances in film making become propaganda weapons aimed at instilling hatred toward the "other," while new discoveries in chemistry result in the production of Zyklon B. Had the infamies of WWII taken place five thousand years ago, one might at least be able to argue humanity had "outgrown" such deplorable conduct. But the fact that the greatest carnage in human history occurred within living memory speaks volumes as to how truly limited our spiritual evolution has been. In particular, we must bear in mind the fact that the saurian brain stem is alive and well and, as a result, we must guard against the tendency to confuse technological progress with human progress. The remarkable array of toys and gadgets we continue to produce does not necessarily signal a profound new sapience on the part of Homo sapiens. In fact, it may be contributing to the obverse in the sense that these devices may be fostering a critical misconception confusing technological prowess and wisdom. Most assuredly, these are not the same thing, and failure to perceive the difference clearly can result in devastating miscalculation.

What exactly are we referring to when we speak of wisdom? Let's begin by explaining what it is not. The mere accumulation of data, no matter how cleverly compiled or readily accessible, does not constitute wisdom. Wisdom is not about amassing encyclopedic information. The scientists to whom I referred at the beginning, now possess a thousand times more information than Galileo did in the 16th century, but that in no way guarantees modern scientists are one wit more wise than the Florentine. Wisdom also needs to be distinguished from inventiveness. Creativity, ingenuity, the ability to solve a puzzle or meet some challenge successfully are not necessarily indications of wisdom. The automobile mechanic who can correctly diagnose a fuel injection problem by simply listening to the engine may be a wizard when it comes to auto repair, but wise? Not on this evidence.

How then are we using the term "wisdom"? What I am suggesting here is a kind of Gestalt comprised of intellectual, psychological, and spiritual insights that collectively produce a qualitative whole beyond the sum of the parts. This state of mind comes about, if it comes about at all, only after a long and deliberate attempt to make sense of life. It is not the possession of youth, although the folly of youth often argues the contrary. Nor is it something guaranteed to those who acquire a raft of academic credentials. A PhD does not even immunize against asininity, much less assure wisdom. In terms of wisdom's substance, I view it as the ability to view life clear and whole, as a kind of master "skill" that allows a person to rub the dust from his or her eyes, enjoying thereby the blessings of a properly prioritized existence. Be it hoped you understand that what I am describing here is something categorically distinct from science, industry, or technology. Whoever unmasks the mystery of cold fusion will surely earn the appellation "brilliant physicist," but even in a case such as this there will be no surety of wisdom. Science can provide us with means, with methods, with techniques. It cannot supply us with the governing logic by which we arrive at ends, with the insights by which we attain the larger measures of life. That is to say, a science uninformed by wisdom may not only lead to philistinism; it might even result in a kind of techno-barbarism.

I believe these distinctions are of capital significance and that there are serious potential problems if we fail to consider them. For one thing, I sense an increasing tendency on the part of many people to assume that the on-going accumulation of data is "proof" of humanity's progress and that this avalanche of information, in and of itself, foretells a bright and blissful future. I doubt if anyone would quibble with the idea that information is an indispensable ingredient in rational decision making. However, this logic begs a very important question, viz., by what criteria will this data be organized, on what basis will we separate the informational wheat from the chaff? In other words, how will the directing principles that lend meaning and purpose to raw data materialize? I think too many have come to assume that the answer here somehow emerges spontaneously from the data itself. But the process in question is a bit more complicated than that, and, moreover, a failure to appreciate this complexity could have wide-scale inimical effects. Imagine a situation in which there is a seemingly unlimited capacity to amass data coupled with an inverse capacity to manage it. What are the implications? The first, and most obvious one is the real potential that we may drown in this flood, that the volume of information may become so chaotically overwhelming that, rather than help us solve our problems, it may itself become a source of acute dysfunction. Whenever I consider the possibility of something like this, I am reminded of a term you are not likely to encounter again in your life. The word is *enantiodromia*—a real mouthful. In Greek, the word means "running in opposite ways" and was coined by the psychologist C.G. Jung, although the concept is actually traceable to the sibylline musings of the philosopher Heraclitus. What this peculiar locution suggests is that there is a tendency for things to change into their opposites, that a superabundance of anything will eventually result in a contrary state. In principle, information should have a beneficial effect upon the human condition, but the simple accumulation of data on an immense scale in the absence of guiding precepts represents a real opportunity for the paradoxical recoil suggested by Heraclitus. A mammoth glut of information may not only fail to make our lives easier and more comprehensible, it may actually serve to compound opacity and confusion. Worse still, the anarchic accumulation of data almost certainly will make it more difficult to distinguish relevant information from the superfluous drivel that increasingly litters the information highway. In the absence of evaluative principles, this situation virtually guarantees qualitative bewilderment. So how do we arrive at the assessment capacities needed to navigate this ocean of unrefined data? Here we encounter a rather disquieting circularity. The remedy for all of this lies with those discriminating capacities we have collectively termed "wisdom," but since the development of wisdom is at least in part reliant upon judiciously assayed information, we have a situation in which the presumptive cure for modernity's many ills (data), makes the genuine cure (wisdom), increasingly difficult to attain. Not only does the qualitatively ungoverned accumulation of information lack the capacity to generate its own over-arching insights, it may actually obscure the serviceable data to such a degree that prospects for achieving wisdom are actually diminished—*enantio-dromia* with a vengeance.

In addition to these limitations, modern science and technology may also be responsible for a far more troubling mindset. I like to refer to this as the "masters of the universe syndrome," where people turgidly assert their command of life in all of its multifarious complexity. According to this mindset, there is no problem, threat, or challenge we can't conquer, given enough time and resource. Even death, it is argued, is not a genuine obstacle in view of our limitless capacities, so one would be well advised to reserve space at the nearest cryogenics facility—liquid nitrogen anyone? What we need to consider here is the substance of these boasts. What do they really say about us as human beings? Specifically, we should ask if this Panglossian assessment of human potential is in any sense accurate. Certainly, it is impossible not to be impressed with the record of humanity's achievements to date. A few years ago I recall viewing some images from the Hubble Space Telescope on the evening news. These shots were simply spectacular, and I remember thinking to myself that they were a kind of certificate of "arrival" for the human race. Here we were, a nascent species from a ridiculously insignificant planet prying open the mystery and magic of the universe. A bit of self-congratulatory indulgence seemed fully appropriate. But as the news broadcast continued, my sense of pride and joy in being a member of the hominid family was completely shattered. In the span of just a few minutes I found myself stunned by a stark juxtaposition. One moment I was viewing photos of the Orion Nebula the next, I was looking at rows of body bags in Afghanistan. The conclusion I drew from this was simple, Icarian wings tend to melt. Yes, we are entitled to a sense of accomplishment with regard to our scientific endeavors, but before we all toss our caps into the air, we need to address the continued presence of our inner-Neanderthal. How can one claim the status of master of the universe when mastery of self remains unachieved? How does one reconcile the mapping of the human genome with the hideous reality that man remains wolf to man?

Whenever I consider these questions, I am ineluctably drawn to the insights of classical antiquity. The ancients may not have been able to put objects into earth's orbit, but when it comes to an undistorted understanding of the human condition, their ideas can still shed important light. The ancient Greeks and Romans were powerfully impressed with man's potential to accomplish remarkable things, but at the same time, they never lost sight of humankind's infinite capacity for self-inflicted wounds. In great measure, this explains the peculiar melancholy that continuously oppressed their worldview (e.g. Silenus's advice to King Midas that it is best for a mortal not to be born, but if already born to die as soon as possible). In this regard, the ancients devised a kind of cautionary formula aimed at reminding us that insolent self-satisfaction comes with a price. Specifically, they admonished those with a penchant for *hubris* (arrogance) that they would suffer the effects of *ate* (blindness) which in turn would unleash a vengeful *nemesis* (destructive fate). There are some insights that have a unique capacity to surmount the particularities of time and place and this may be one of them. The genuinely wise are immune from the calamitous sequence of hubris-ate-nemesis not because they possess vast stores of information or because they have the ability to solve technical challenges. They are spared because they understand the true substance of wisdom lies in humility, in an uninflated sense of self that includes consideration of the dark shades that continue to vex the human spirit.

In sum, while I am by no means a neo-Luddite, I nevertheless strongly advocate the distinction between wisdom and technological achievement. Moreover, understand that the latter has increasingly revealed an ability to confuse and obscure the meaning of the former, a capacity from which, I suspect, no good can come.

Understand, too, that in the absence of wisdom we become little more than children who can't be trusted to play with their toys properly—a danger to ourselves and the world in which we live. Finally, recognize that no consideration along these lines can be properly formulated without contemplating the perennial difficulties presented by the excesses of human ego. It seems no laboratory exploit, no space probe, no investigation of sub-atomic particles can put a dent in man's lust for vaunting swagger. Would you like an image for all this? Imagine a peacock—chest pompously swollen, plumage bombastically displayed, and a strut that unmistakably conveys imperious vanity. Yes, there is a sense in which we can agree with the portrait of man as "earth's little god." However, this is a little god that still needs to sleep with the lights on, because the ancient specters continue to haunt his existence and will do so unendingly until such time as scientific proficiency is guided and informed by the larger considerations associated with the term wisdom.

On What You Owe Your Fellow Human Being

We live in a time and place where many assume little if anything is owed our fellow human beings. A variety of powerful forces, both intellectual and economic, have conspired to create and reinforce this impression. Even a most casual reading of philosophers such as Machiavelli, Hobbes and Locke suggests that self-interest is the overarching motive of human conduct and that societal institutions must be structured and organized to reflect this persistent reality. Even the founders of our Republic were strongly inclined in this direction. Madison, for instance, understood that arriving at anything approximating the public good was an exceedingly difficult challenge given the fact that the latent causes of faction are "sown in the nature of man" (Federalist #10). These same assumptions also comprise the foundational logic for much of the capitalist system. The raw energy that propels the free market is the competitive instinct of the self-regarding entrepreneur. Capitalism is a rivalrous model that tends neither to acknowledge nor reward cooperative endeavor. In the business arena one owes the competitor little, perhaps not even a principled transaction. These, I suspect, are the sorts of viewpoints that have encouraged people to assume that they have no real duties or obligations to their fellow human beings. Their responsibilities extend no further than themselves and an immediate, narrow circle of friends and family. Beyond these parameters, "humanity" constitutes a kind of abstract "other" with which one need not be concerned.

Now, of course, there are some happy exceptions to what I have just written but I do suspect the majority of people typically subscribe to some version of "not my problem" when it comes to issues of larger social obligation. To what extent are these sentiments valid, and, more specifically, to what degree are the assumptions of man's inherent self-absorption accurate? In raising this issue we immediately find ourselves face to face with one of the most vexing questions ever advanced, viz, How are we to understand human nature? This is hardly a new question. It has intrigued and confounded humankind for literally thousands of years and even now we are still not in a position to offer a definitive assessment. What we can say with some certainty is that who and what we are as human beings is a mysterious combination of nature and nurture, a hybrid of biological and environmental variables. The great difficulty lies in designating which category constitutes the ultimate ingredient in determining human identity. If you ask a behavioral psychologist like B.F. Skinner, the answer is "nurture," but if you ask a biologist such as James Watson, the answer is likely to be "nature." Our efforts to assess the alleged egocentrism of man, the logic by which we might justify non-concern for one's fellows, are, by their very nature, shaped by this enduring question of genetics versus environment. I do not presume for one moment to possess some prescient insight in these matters, but I can offer what I believe is a reasonable hypothesis.

Evolutionary biology is an essential framework in any attempt to make sense of human behavior—both individually and collectively. In other words, it is fully reasonable to speak of a genetic code, a kind of behavioral program, buried deep within us. The presence of this code is no doubt related to its survival benefits. In essence, we are hardwired to respond to certain threats and challenges in ways that will enhance our prospects for continued existence. This may include selfish acts or even acts of violence depending on circumstances. But the key point here is these reactions are elicited responses. They are triggered by environmental circumstance; they are not spontaneous secretions indicative of uncontrollable savagery. In other words, we must not think in terms of simple reflex when we consider the baffling complexities of human conduct. A good deal of biological programming comes into play in response to environmental cues, but man is uniquely capable of configuring his world, meaning that he has in principle, the ability to control many of the signals that occasion less than enviable responses. I suspect most people would agree our biological profile includes potential for both good and evil. The real question is what the social and cultural contingencies are requisite for the support of the former and the suppression of the latter.

It seems to me cultural setting is a very important factor in all of this. Like most things in life, culture is capable of advancing either benign or malignant objectives. On the positive side, culture is able to preserve and convey humanity's most precious attainments in areas such as art, literature, science, music, etc. In this regard, it represents a most valuable parsimony to the extent it spares us the time and energy of having to recreate and rediscover. At the same time, however, this transfer of priceless legacy can also include a good deal of dross. In addition to endowing us with the highest and the best, culture also tends to transmit much that is false, crude, absurd and outrageously mindless. In doing so, society and culture are in a position to call forth behavioral responses that might otherwise remain latent potentials only. I do not question for one moment that there is a darkness in the human heart; history is depressingly replete with illustrations of this. Still, I believe society and culture must be held responsible for their roles in making manifest much of this ugliness, and I also believe attempts to dismiss depraved conduct by appealing to trite phrases like "such is the nature of man" are nothing more than disingenuous copouts. We may have the potential to swindle, betray and violently mistreat our fellow human beings but these evils are not inevitable features of the human condition. To some significant degree, they are summoned to the behavioral surface by society's tacit endorsement of values and institutions that support such practices. If, for example, a society's economic, political, and educational systems encourage and reward predatory mentalities one cannot legitimately assign the resulting behavior exclusively to genetic determinism. Some might argue, of course, that the institutions and values in question are themselves reflections of biologically ordained negatives, that they simply mirror inexorable tendencies for degenerate behavior. The problem with this reasoning is that it implies man is little more than a helpless marionette incapable of resisting the tyranny of a few strands of DNA. Not only does this view falsely discount our species' demonstrated capacity to vary the script Mother Nature has written for us, it also tends to support the notion that the misanthrope is a natural and fitting representative of the species. So, in response to the idea that we should resign ourselves to the logic of "such is the nature of man," I would answer, yes, such is man's nature but only after culture and society have reinforced a radical neglect of moral and social alternatives.

Let us now return to our original question: what do we owe our fellow human beings? The short answer is more than we have been led to assume. Once we accept the idea that we are not indentured to aboriginal urges, that we are thinking, choosing, judging creatures capable of exercising a higher freedom, we begin to run out of excuses for treating people as if they were means to our personal ends. These same cognitive assets also allow us to unmask a pernicious series of societal premises that seek to advance inhumanity as a natural and fitting expression of our genetic makeup. No matter how many times we hear these arguments, and they will often be proffered as a kind of self-evident gospel, one must resist the temptation to accept these views. About the last thing this world needs right now is more advocates of social Darwinism. What it needs, instead, is a sincerely held conviction that humanity—all humanity—is worthy and good and that time spent seeking out and cultivating this goodness is the highest expression of one's own value and merit. Now, of course, you understand the limitations inherent in what I am suggesting. Your efforts alone will not cure the world's ills and you will most assuredly encounter individuals in whom your faith in the fundamental decency of humanity is poorly demonstrated. Nevertheless, make it your business to do nothing that might add to the pain and suffering of your fellow human being. Conquer your instincts for reprisal and penalty. Even when you enjoy a legal prerogative to inflict retribution, abstain from doing so. Never forget that justice is a loaf best leavened with mercy. In all such matters, think of the ancient rabbis and always choose to sit at the compassionate knee of Hillel rather than invoke the juridical strictures of Shammai. Above all, make of yourself a dwelling place for things generous, benign, and magnanimous. In doing this, you will not only be making some small contribution to improving the human condition, you will also be enriching your own life. And one final point. Never forget the virtue of well spent tears. More than anything else, it is our tears that demonstrate our humanity, that prove both our superiority to and distance from the primordial muck from which we evolved. So if at some point in your life you find yourself capable of offering up a few salty droplets for your fellow man or woman, even for those with whom you have little or no relation, rejoice in the knowledge that your soul is ripe and that you have achieved some degree of your calling as a human being.

Zeus's Urns

In the final book of Homer's *Iliad*, there is a powerful scene in which Achilles and Priam, the Trojan king, mourn the terrible losses each has suffered in the war. Both men are gripped by an overwhelming grief but soon Achilles recomposes himself and observes that in the end, no advantage can "be won from grim lamentation." He then goes on to fatalistically describe the crucible the gods have ordained for humankind. Unlike the Olympians, who know no grief, humanity is destined to "live in unhappiness" because Zeus bestows human destiny from two urns: an urn of evils and an urn of blessings. Some individuals will receive a measure from each vessel with the result their lives will oscillate between interludes of joy and anguish. Others less fortunate receive an allotment exclusively drawn from the urn of sorrows. They will experience a life of unrelenting misery without prospect of relief. Significantly, Achilles offers no description of an individual assigned a life of unmixed blessing. Homer's message is clear: There are no charmed lives, no immunities from the trials of human existence. The most one can expect according to Achilles' account is a life of wrenching swings—one moment laughter, the next, tears.

Homer's description of the fate that awaits humanity offers a revealing portrait of how the ancient Greeks understood the human condition. Few people in history were more inclined to celebrate the joys of life, but, at the same time, few were more disposed to recognize periods of merriment as tenuous and fleeting, brief interludes between more telling moments of anguish and pain. This explains the muted despair that seems to underscore so much of their culture, and it undoubtedly prompted the investigations of human suffering presented on the tragic stage. In my view, these sentiments constitute an enduring wisdom which Western culture has assiduously sought to discredit or deny. Admittedly, life's dreadful uncertainties are, to say the least, intimidating, and one can fully understand modernity's preference for rejecting the trauma of existence. To their credit, the ancients, with few exceptions, tended to favor a more unvarnished view of such questions. They were much less inclined to ignore human vulnerability, and, more specifically, they forthrightly rejected notions that divine rescue was a serious possibility. Moreover, the ancients were similarly disinclined to assume human enterprise might somehow reverse the malignant verdicts of fortune. We, on the other hand, have chosen a less resolute path. Some of us embrace various religious assurances that promise exemption from life's untoward episodes, while others insist there is a curative to be found in human endeavor, that exponential increases in man's scientific and technological capacities will soon allow us to dictate the terms of our own destiny. I respectfully submit, both of these positions are misguided and reflect an all too human propensity to manufacture separate "truths" in the face of distasteful reality.

With regard to deliverance from on High, the Judeo-Christian tradition promises that a solicitous and all-powerful God is piloting the universe and that we, as his children, are in good and generous hands. Terms such as fate, destiny, fortune, to the extent they indicate blind uncertainties beyond control or calculation, wither in the presence of divine providence. Our world, we are assured, is a benignly governed domain in which justice and righteousness ultimately prevail—God does not roll dice, nor does he permit them to be rolled. These are comforting thoughts, and their appeal remains strong even in a secular age. A recent survey, for example, reveals that more than fifty percent of Americans believe in guardian angels and that these views are even held by some who have no religious affiliation whatsoever. Still, conviction is no guarantee of truth, and, as a result, it is incumbent upon all reasoning men and women to weigh the validity of such beliefs, particularly in light of so much countervailing evidence.

With respect to God's merciful administration of the universe, the faithful are confronted with a highly inconvenient fact, viz., the abundance of evil in the world. If, indeed, God is a good and all-powerful steward, then how is it that so much of the world seems to be a bungled job? Religious authorities have devised a variety of explanations to address this matter, none of which seem particularly satisfying. Chief among these, at least in the Western tradition, is a teaching that aims to attach responsibility for life's ills to man himself. This involves the ingenious doctrine of free-will where, we are told, God graciously awarded us a special capacity, the ability to determine the course and substance of our own lives. From the outset, however, as illustrated by the sin of Adam, we are told humanity was inclined to corrupt and misapply this liberty with the result that we utterly confounded the paradisiac intentions of God. In other words, the world is broken (evil), and we have only ourselves to blame for its state of disrepair. And so, as we scan the record of history and find ourselves shocked by a seemingly infinite roster of horrors and cruelties, the theologians argue these are to be understood as the malignant fruits of mismanaged free will.

In addition to begging a variety of questions, this theodicy seems disproportionately exculpatory in favor of God. While few would deny the savage darkness of the human heart or the appalling ease with which we are inclined to dismiss the cries of the innocent, the list of human shortcomings still fails to exonerate God fully. Rather than extend God a free-pass in these matters, we need to ask how a good, loving, all powerful deity can remain on the sidelines in the face of abject injustice. Again, the fault may be ours, but godly indifference in the presence of something like genocide raises some rather disquieting questions about divine identity and motive. It would seem that God is either incapable of preventing evil, in which case he is not all-powerful, or he is unwilling to do so, in which case he is not all-good.

The second way in which we have strayed from Homeric insight involves an inflated view of human capacity. This point has been touched upon in part in chapter thirteen. It concerns the arrogant and dubious assumptions that human enterprise is capable of solving every problem, curing every infirmity, removing every obstacle, thereby exempting us from life's myriad ills. The source of this self-congratulatory optimism is, no doubt, a combination of our remarkable scientific accomplishments and the imaginative energies of the advertising industry that urges us to see a glass not only as half full but as positively overflowing with the result that we are all encouraged to eat, drink, and be merry (i.e. consume). But how true are the assurances that man has the ability to minimize evil and guarantee blessing? Are we now truly able to ensure distribution exclusively from the urn of joy? In considering these questions we are confronted by another form of evil, one unrelated to human deficiency. For lack of a better term, let us refer to this other category as "irrational evil," by which I mean an ontological malevolence, an evil embedded in existence itself. This is what Albert Camus was alluding to when he observed that "the world is absurd," meaning that the world does what it wants with depraved indifference to man's "wild longing for clarity." As rational creatures we have an abiding need for lucidity, meaning, and purpose. But what if there is a profound and incomprehensible disconnect between our desires to decipher the world and the world's willingness to be deciphered?

What if existence is inherently false, cruel, contradictory, and meaningless with the result that affliction and misery are randomly distributed among innocent and guilty alike? How does one guarantee blessing in an environment where irrational contingency is prepared to operate with callous disregard for human agency? By way of illustration, just remind yourself of the "fate" of those who died on 9/11. It is impossible to understand these deaths as in any way justifiable or merited. The evil that so rudely claimed their lives reveals a simple and horrifying truth: wrong place, wrong time and nothing anyone or anything can do will spare your life.

All of this brings us back to Zeus's two urns and the *Iliad's* sober realism. Homer was right to remind us that, try as we might to evade the brute reality of human existence, there is no shelter from the storm we call life. Paternosters and technology notwithstanding, our existence remains bound to a cruel uncertainty in light of which the hoped-for benefactions of God and human ingenuity seem fatuous indeed. How, then, shall we conduct ourselves in view of these gloomy prospects? Be it noted, I am not suggesting we abandon all hope or that we resign ourselves to some wretched, joyless existence. Nor am I urging the abandonment of scientific endeavor as part of our admission that the great existential questions are beyond the capacity of science to resolve. And, again, I do not advocate a general renunciation of religious belief. The faithful are entitled to their prayers but they are also entitled to their doubts. As rational beings we have a right, if not an obligation, to challenge indemonstrable nostrums, to question, dispute, and appraise critically every uncertified social convention and religious premise. Loyalties in these matters should never be blind, nor should they serve as a rationale for mental truancy. Readers are encouraged, therefore, to cling to their doubts and to understand that these uncertainties, as unnerving as they may be, are a precious human asset by which the species has marked much of its progress. Finally, I urge readers to approach life as eminently worthy of yea-saying. The grammar of life may indeed include a wanton absurdity that mocks our yearning for order and meaning but, in the end, we must still conclude that life is a good and beautiful thing and something that fully merits clear-eyed affirmation.

CPSIA information can be obtained
at www.ICGtesting.com
Printed in the USA
BVOW06s0115301217

504000BV00004B/139/P